T0365874

# MY STORY BY YEARS

## THE LIFE AND TIMES OF
## JULIUS NEAL CLEMMER

### Lt. Col. USAF (Ret.)

*I dedicate this book to my Grandmother*
*Rhoda Elisabeth McKenzie Lear*
*For she made me what I am, and have been.*

Copyright © 2003 by Julius Neal Clemmer. 534896

All rights reserved. No part of this book may
be reproduced or transmitted in any form or by
any means, electronic or mechanical, including
photocopying, recording, or by any information storage
and retrieval system, without permission in writing from
the copyright owner.

To order additional copies of this book, contact:
Xlibris
844-714-8691
www.Xlibris.com
Orders@Xlibris.com

ISBN:   Softcover        978-1-4134-1498-1
        Hardcover        978-1-4134-6117-6

Library of Congress Control Number:     2003093949

Print information available on the last page

Rev. date: 01/26/2023

Forward:

This is about the sixth or seventh time that I have started this program. I have tried the narrative approach; however, that did not seem to work. I would remember a time or an event that needed to be inserted into the text. I found that very hard to do. Now I've hit upon the idea of doing it by years. This is quite an undertaking as it will have to cover some eighty years.

The names and places mentioned in this book are real. But the dates of certain events may not be accurate

Now I will start with the year 1923.

# CHAPTER I

# The First Decade

1923. This all began on January 26th. All I know about that day is on my birth certificate. The certificate states that I was born to Colinetta Lear Clemmer and Julius Neal Clemmer.

However, there is a picture that was taken when I was six months old. It seems my grandmother said, "If no one else will take a picture of this child, I will." She dressed me, up took me to the photographer and here is the result.

1924. These are some of the pictures that I think were taken about this time. Other than them I have no memory of the 1924.

1925. This seems to be a picture of me in front of Grandmother's house. It was about this time that they had to fence the back yard. The reason for fencing was that I had started to roam. The picture below is of my grandfather Lear with Betty and me in the wheelbarrow. With Grandmother Lear, I looked to be in the terrible twos.

1926. By this year we were playing with the neighborhood children, one of whom was Keith Wayne Nelson. Keith and I were friends for many years. It was on my third birthday when I received a tricycle. The delivery man

brought it to the door and I immediately got on to ride and rode into the dining room table. With that my mother put me back down to take a nap.

The sad fact is that the trike outlasted my mother.

Judging from my size, I would have to guess that I was probably three years old when this picture was taken. It was on the Will Brooks farm, west of Whiting, Iowa.

1927. I have a vague recollection that something significant happened during this time. My friend Keith was born in St. Louis, Missouri, and there was a connection to that and the Spirit of St. Louis. I had no idea what it meant to fly an airplane or what the Atlantic Ocean was about. Later in life, I was to fly airplanes and cross the Atlantic Ocean eighteen times as of this writing.

It was during these years that we went barefoot during the summer. In the fall we went downtown Omaha to buy new shoes. When your mother thought you had a good fit, they would put your feet into a fluoroscope to see where the toe bones came in reference to the end of the shoe. It is a wonder that we all don't have foot problems from all the X-rays.

At this time, when all mothers stayed home, they had the service of home delivery, the milk was left at the door every day (in glass bottles), and the bakery man came with the baked goods. The interesting thing is that they came in horse-drawn wagons. The horses knew the customers and stopped at the right houses every time. If the delivery man walked to the next house, he would whistle and the horse would go to the next house and stop.

1928. This is the fall when my formal education began My kindergarten teacher had had my mother as a student. The school was Saratoga, and our colors were green and white. Every fall we get new pen wipers for the top of the ink bottle. It was a square of green felt on the bottom, a smaller square of white felt cloth on the top, held in place on the cork of the ink bottle with a thumb tack. The inkwell was located on the upper right-hand corner of the desk. Everyone was supposed to be right handed, including me; however, I picked the pen up with my left hand. This was a no-no. So at an early age I was converted to being right handed. Perhaps that has had something to do with my dyslexia.

It was during this time when my aunt Eleanor married Arthur Graham and brought the Graham children into our lives.

Also about this time we were living with Grandmother Lear on Twenty-fourth Street. My other grandparents the Clemmers lived on Saratoga Street, which was only a few blocks away. It was my habit to frequently visit Saratoga. One summer day I went in to the house on Saratoga and on the floor on a blanket was a baby. I asked Grandmother Clemmer, "Whose baby is this?" She replied, "It's your uncle Bob's." With this great piece of information, I ran home to spread the good news.

I arrived home and told my mother and my grandmother that Uncle Bob had a baby. I was immediately informed that Uncle Bob did not have a baby. The reason given was

that he was not married. It was many years later that this "baby" contacted me for information about our family. I knew immediately it was the "baby" whom I had seen at Grandmother Clemmer's house. No one else in the family was aware of her. We made contact and I saw her several times before she died.

This is my cousin Jackie, with her husband "Doc," and the author and his wife Mary Jane.

1929. The stock market crashed this year but I have no recollection of the events that took place. As for any outstanding memories of 1929, I have one. My first grade teacher, Bess Howard, was a great woman who stood over six feet and for a six-year-old she was a giant. I met her again in 1945 and will cover that later.

It was during this period of our lives when we spent many happy Sundays picnicking. After church the picnic basket was packed and off we went into the country. My father would find a nice spot with shade and, hopefully, running water and we would lay out Sunday dinner and picnic. This went on even in the cold winter. I well remember one cold picnic with snow on the ground and ice in the stream bed that we broke out with our feet. Also, it must've been during this period that my mother acquired a mastoid infection. She was operated on by the famous Dr. Maxwell, and apparently a bone chip went down the Eustachian tube. The bone chip lodged in her lung, creating abscesses. The doctor had dated my aunt Elenore, and was called three times to sew up my chin. Once, I was told, he arrived on a motorcycle. In the 1920s that was a real no-no for a doctor. The good

doctor had hunted in Africa, and had lion skins on his wall. After his trip to India, he came home with two tiger skins as well. I was greatly impressed!

1930. Life went on and school started the day after Labor Day as always. Going to school was never my favorite pastime. During these years we went to visit the Brooks families in Iowa on many occasions. The Brooks' had farms west of Whiting, Iowa. As I write this, there is only one Brooks left. That is Eila.

1931. This year draws a complete blank. I do remember that my mother had only one good ear and was sick a lot.

This is the only family picture that I have, and it came from my cousin Jackie.

1932. It was in May of this year when my mother died. The whole family was in shock. I believe this picture was taken in Whiting, Iowa, after my mother had died. As you may have noticed, Betty and I are bigger in this picture, and also I never remember my grandmother Lear going to Iowa while my mother was alive. From the left are my father, Aunt

Rose Brooks, Grandmother Lear, Aunt Edith Brooks, Uncle Will Brooks, and Eila Brooks. Betty and I are in front.

The Depression was in full swing, people had no jobs and no money, and the future looked bad.

In November, my father went to a Spanish club in Omaha and met a lady who was from Mexico. She had married an American, with whom she had two daughters before her husband died of tularemia. My father and she decided that marriage would be the ideal situation for both of them. As it turned out, the union only lasted nine years. The poor woman had no idea that she was about to take on an uncivilized boy. To her credit, I owe her a great debt of gratitude. She had the daunting task of trying to instill something in the way of table manners. She also made my first-ever dental appointment, for that I still have my teeth. To her credit she was an avid opera buff. So I was introduced to classical music at an early age.

# — CHAPTER II —
# The Second Decade

1933. The new family soon moved to Hampton, Iowa, where father built an ice plant. Looking back, I wonder why he would choose northern Iowa as a place on which to build an ice plant. God knows it is cold there most of the time. For you who have never known anything but artificial refrigeration, there was a time when ice was the only way to cool your food.

The old saying is that every man has his woman, but the iceman has his pick. This is because the iceman brought ice to the house and put it in the top of the ice box.

If the homeowner only needed a small amount, the iceman would use his pick to cut a small piece. He would then carry the ice in the house and there was a sign in the window that told him how much to deliver.

When ice melts, the water must be contained. To do this, there was a pan under the ice box. Someone had to empty the pan at regular intervals, and when one forgot there was a mop job to be done.

My most vivid memory of this year was attending school. The elementary school in Hampton, Iowa, was built sometime in the 1800s. It was a large brick building with four classrooms on the main floor and four classrooms on the second floor. There was a large wooden stairway in the middle of the building, and the classrooms on the second floor were off a balcony.

For fire escapes, there were large tubes from each second-floor classroom to the ground. Twice every year we had a fire drill-one in the spring and one in the fall. The routine was this: One boy, who was wearing a pair of sturdy pants (to clear the dust and bugs), was selected. He was the first down the slide, then he must step to the side and look away because the girls were the next to come down the fire escape. The boys would then be allowed to slide down.

Another happening of interest this year was the repeal of the Prohibition. For the first time in many years, one could purchase alcohol legally. There was a liquor store that opened in Hampton and one of the first customers was my father.

During these tough years I had a paper route for the Des Moines Register and Tribune. The paper boy collected the money for the subscription, and trying to get fifteen cents each week was real work. Early one very cold and snowy Sunday morning, the papers were late in arriving from Des Moines. One of the paper boys said, "Let's go have breakfast." That was a great idea, but where? He led us to a soup kitchen down by the railroad tracks where the bums and hobos were eating. There we had pancakes and coffee. The papers arrived and I delivered my route. Upon arriving home I was asked if I wanted breakfast. I said, "No, I had already eaten." When I told them where, I was immediately scrubbed and my clothes were boiled as if I had been exposed to every disease known to man. Perhaps I had, but it was a great experience.

1934. Two of my memories from this time are as follows. The better memory is my father's purchase of a new Ford automobile. This is the first automobile I ever drove at the ripe old age of eleven.

Of the second memory, I have a very pungent memory. It's from a class project where you had a partner to work on a problem. My partner was from an immigrant family and his mother had sewn him into his long underwear. You'll have to understand that this sewing took place in the fall of the year. By March the poor kid had not been out of his underwear once. To say you could smell him a mile away is not an exaggeration. This was in an era when Lifebuoy soap was being advertised to prevent BO (body odor).

In the fall of 1934, I went into the sixth grade, which was junior high. I had a new bike that fall with the money that I had earned over the summer. Father had installed a root beer stand at his ice plant. We had the big glass mugs, trays that we would fit on the window of the car, and ice cream. We sold a mug of ice cold root beer for five cents, and an ice cream cone was the same, so a root beer float came to ten cents. One thin dime!

1935. The winter of 1935 was very bad. It was so cold that they couldn't keep the school heated, so we had a long series of "snow days." At one time the temperature dropped to negative thirty-five degrees Fahrenheit. In fact, the cold and snow stopped the railroad trains, as they could not keep up the steam to run them.

The times were looking better; my father sold the ice plant. He got his old job back at the Baker Ice Machine Co. in Omaha, and we moved back to Omaha too. I was in the seventh grade, back in elementary school at Saratoga with my original classmates.

However, I had to attend summer school in order to keep up with my class.

1936. The highlight of this year was my father's trip to the Philippines. He was the first paying passenger on the China clipper to Manila. He went there to install air-conditioner at the Manila Hotel. It was the first building in the city to be air-conditioned. Somehow, I finished the seventh grade and was promoted to the eighth grade. For P.E. we played soccer as that was considered best for our age. Now they start at two years of age.

This was another eventful year. We were living in a house on Ames Avenue in Omaha that had been a house of ill repute. This caused some

rather interesting phone calls, and visits. It was much later that I became aware of what had happened. This is the house.

I did get to suit up for a baseball game in the spring, but didn't get in the game until the ninth inning. End of career.

In June I graduated from Saratoga and went on to high school at North High in the fall. Shortly after school, we (the six of us) took off for New York City. My father had purchased a 1937 Ford with a sixty horsepower motor. The car was so under-powered you had to avoid a wad of gum, or call a tow truck. The reason for the trip was for my father to see about a job with the Carrier Co. He got the job, and we moved to Syracuse, New York.

There I entered junior high again. In the spring I was promoted to high school for the final time. Every move we had made over the years meant a different grade level. In Iowa I went from grade school to junior high; we moved to Omaha, and I was back in elementary. Then I went to North High School, but in Syracuse it was back to junior high, then high school at last.

As we were living in the Snow Belt, I learned to ski, play hockey and lacrosse. I never would have played all sports if we had stayed in Omaha.

1938. This year I had another paper route. There did not seem to be any outstanding event. My father did finish his training with Carrier and was sent to Mexico. He drove to Mexico in a 1939 Chevrolet.

1939. With plans for the family to move to Mexico, my sister Betty wrote to Grandmother Lear and requested that she finish high school in America. My father agreed. Unbeknownst to me, Grandmother Lear asked that I come with Betty to finish school too. As my father's marriage was crumbling, he agreed that I could go to Omaha also. Betty and I were put on the train for Chicago where we had to change stations for the trip to Omaha. Betty graduated from North High in June and I finished my sophomore year there also.

On June 11, 1939, I received Holy Confirmation in St. John's Episcopal Church.

That fall I went out to my Uncle Ray's (my dads' oldest brother) farm to help my cousin Darrel harvest the corn crop. Now we weren't riding in one of today's big air-conditioned combines, we did it the old-fashioned way-by hand. Darrel would get the team of horses from the barn, put on their harness, hook up the tongue, tighten the double tree, climb up on the wagon seat, slap the reins, and with a "gitty up" the horses would start forward. With that first hard pull on the wagon, the horses would break wind, and as we moved along they would pass more gas. Looking for a better way to put this un-delicate subject I went to the thesaurus and there was a great four-letter word that described it to a tee, "fart." Count yourselves lucky that you never sat on a

hard wagon seat in the early morning behind a two horse-powered fart!

Once we got to the corn field, it was all work. You had to remove the husks, bare the ear of corn so you cold break it off, and toss it into the wagon. There were two ways of removing the husks: One was the husking hook, and the other was to use a husking peg. You attach the peg or hook to either hand to separate the husks. With my hook in place, I took the inside row of corn closest to the wagon. Darrel took the outside row, and we were off for the day. We tried to keep one ear from hitting the bang board in a steady rhythm as the horses walked along. The "bang board" is just a high side on the wagon so that you don't miss the wagon by overthrowing an ear.

1940. In my junior year at North High, I enrolled in the drama class. We studied about lighting, acting, stage presence, and makeup. For the spring show I helped with the makeup for the various acts. It was great fun. I was also in the Army Junior ROTC program. With a war in Europe getting imminent, we knew we would have to serve sooner or later. In fact the ROTC training did serve me well when I entered the army.

I was in a Sea Scout Ship with many of my friends this year. We all had sailor suits with bellbottom trousers and coats of navy blue, and everything else was very nautical. We even had a mock-up of a sailing ship on the bank of Carter Lake. The first step in watercraft was the rowboat, then the canoe, and finally the sailboat. Sailing was the best of all, and I kept it up as long as I was in Omaha.

The "ship" was called the LCOOR as the troop was sponsored by the Lutheran Church of our Redeemer. This church was right across the street from our house on North Twenty-fourth Street.

The "ship" was often called on to usher at many civic affairs. One such ushering job was for the Glen Miller Show at the old city auditorium. Glen did his fifteen-minute show for Chesterfield cigarettes. Another time we were asked to usher at the Aksarben (Nebraska spelled backwards) for a performance of Paul Whiteman and his band of renown.

1941. I started school in the fall of 1940, it was my senior year. I have great memories of being at the head of the class, that is age wise, not academics. There were several interesting things that happened during this year in school. I needed an extra one-half credit so I took the Junior Glee Club for freshman boys. Our one public appearance was at Joslyn Memorial Art Museum in Omaha for a Christmas show. I didn't do much singing, but I did handle the makeup for the chorus. I could not take drama in my last semester as I needed a language class. Having heard Spanish spoken all my life, I opted to take Spanish. The Spanish teacher knew both my father and stepmother so the first day in class she asked me to read the first chapter in the book. With all freshmen looking on, I read the entire chapter in Spanish. That was my last good day in Spanish class. It was the only school course that I had ever failed; my father would have killed me had he ever found out. Before the spring show, I was put in charge of all the makeup for every act. I determined who would get a dry (powder) or a wet (grease paint) makeup. All soloists were wet, of course, and the chorus members were made up with dry. My responsibility was to see to it that there was a proper amount of each kind of makeup for the performers. I was not able to take the last semester of drama so I was not in the senior play. I did, however, do the makeup, and the sound effects for the play. On the day of the performance, one of the actors was sent home by the school nurse. I was pressed into service and performed in both the matinee and the evening performance. A week before graduation, the dean of men came to me and

Graduation picture.

said I was one-half a credit short to graduate. That meant not getting my diploma with my friends and having to go to summer school. The members of the drama class each got one-half credit for being in the senior play. Having been in the senior play, I asked for that half credit. The drama teacher agreed to it, that I had indeed earned a half credit, so I graduated on time.

After graduation, I went to work for Western Electric, which was part of AT&T at that time. I was trained as a central office equipment installer. I was working at the telephone company in December when we were attacked by the Japanese.

My grandparents were my role models, during my high school years, as I had neither a father nor a mother.

1942. I was working in Minneapolis, Minnesota, early this year when we all knew we would have to go into military service. After much discussion, it was unanimously decided that becoming an army pilot was the optimum choice. The rationale was that in the navy your boat could be sunk, and any other branch of service leaves you on the ground, in the mud. So the army uniform was best, the officers had the fifty-

mission crushed hats, the green blouse and pink pants (see picture later). So with these lofty ideals in mind I went and joined the army to become an aviation cadet. I took an induction physical at Fort Crook in Bellevue, Nebraska. The day I was taking my physical, standing stark naked, they brought in two busloads of African American draftees. It is a day I will long remember because Thomas Jefferson was wrong: All men are not created equal. I passed both the physical and the aviation cadet examinations. So my military career began in the Enlisted Reserve. I had to wait for an opening in the cadet training program. Some of my friends were called before I received my call. They went into the college training program, which delayed their entrance into the cadet flying program. My official date of entry into the United States Army was on August 10, 1942.

Grandmother Lear and her brother Dave

The Clemmer grandparents

Waiting on my call to active duty.

# — CHAPTER III —
# The Third Decade

1943. I was called to active duty on the fourth of February 1943. So began a military career that lasted for twenty-seven years. Upon being called into service, I reported to the train station and boarded a troop train. Everything being classified, we had no idea where we were heading. The trip ended on the siding of an air base. From the dark of night people were hollering, "You will be sorry," and they were so right. There was a sergeant hollering at us to sign in at 2100 hours, we had no idea what that was, as we had never heard yet of military time. The next day, it was a typical scene handing out uniforms, shoes, equipment, etc., none of which fit. We were in what was called the Classification Center; here you learn to wear the uniform, march in formation, and all the other military necessities. Having had ROTC, I already knew much of this so I was ahead of the rest of the cadets. It was at this time that the determination was made if you would be a pilot, a navigator, or a bombardier.

The physical examinations that were given covered everything from head to toe. I passed all the physical requirements, 20/20 vision, good hearing, great depth perception. However, I fell short on the weight requirement. I had to report to the flight surgeon to schedule a second weight check. The doctor gave me a prescription for bananas and milk. I ate bananas and drank milk until I was about to burst. The next morning a sergeant checked my weight again. I took the results to the flight surgeon, who took a look and said, "We will have to weigh you again." I was about five feet seven inches tall and should have weighed 125 pounds. However, I was a ninety-seven-pound wonder. Fearing that I would not make the weight the second time, I was in a panic. The doctor then took his eraser and changed the weight to the proper figure. He said, "Now you weigh enough." That not only made my day, but my career.

After classification, we went to preflight and this training was basic to all the flying training. I was in Cadet Class 43K. We had learned the Morse Code at five words per minute; this separated many cadets from the program. We had physical education twice each day, given by mean instructors. They worked us very hard, and we ran for miles and miles every day.

Upon completion of preflight, we were on a troop train heading for flying training. We arrived at Fort Stockton, Texas, to take our primary flying training. I took my first flight on May 27, 1943. It was in a Fairchild PT-19A as shown.

After eight hours and forty-six minutes of dual training, I was able to solo. My first of flight alone (solo) was on June 11, 1943, and lasted for a total of seventeen minutes. My final flight in primary was on July 27, which completed my primary flying training. Now it was on the basic training where we flew the BT-13A Vultee as pictured below.

This airplane had a 450-hp engine, a radio, and a full set of instruments. My first flight was on August 17, and I soloed on August 25. My log book indicates that I flew on September 6 for the last time until September 22. The reason for this delay was that I was home on leave because my sister's husband, Lloyd Crapenhoff, had been killed in an airplane accident. That happened at Rose Field in St. Joe, Missouri. Upon my return I could finish the ground school portion of training, but not the flying. So I finished my flying training in basic with Class 44A. My final basic flight was on October 30 and I had acquired 152 hours of flying time.

This is how I looked when I was in basic flying training. I almost didn't make it to this point, which is an interesting story. One evening I got a call that I had a visitor at the front gate. It was a girl I had known while in primary flying school.

While we were talking, my instructor came out of the front gate. She had known him when he was in primary flying school. She would not pay any attention to his calling, so he drove off in a huff. The next day my instructor put me up for a check ride. That was to be the first step in washing me out of the cadet program. I reported for my check ride and a lieutenant said, "Come with me, Cadet," but a major standing nearby said, "I will fly with this cadet." The lieutenant looked daggers at the major, but there was nothing he could do. I flew with the major who said I was a good pilot and asked why I was put up for a check ride. I told them it was a personality conflict and he gave me another instructor. Before any further action to wash me out could be taken, I went on leave to attend the funeral. Upon my return, I was placed in another flight and that ended any further check rides, or threat of washing out. My last flight in basic training was on October 30, 1943.

My advance training began on November 8. I was now flying the AT-6 pictured below.

This plane has a 650-hp engine, and a whole set of instruments, radio, and the addition of a retractable landing gear.

On the December 12th, I flew the P-40 Kittyhawk fighter aircraft for the first time; this was a 500-hp jump to 1100 hp.

My father came to visit me while I was in advanced training. He came with his third wife, Alita, who I met with the first time. This is a picture taken at that time.

Toward the end of our training, the day after Christmas, we flew to Matagorda Island, Texas, for gunnery training. The AT-6 had one .30-caliber machine gun in the right wing. We fired the machine gun at a target towed by another airplane, as shown below.

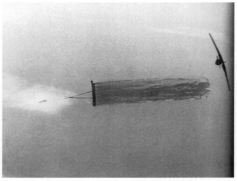

The target was a large piece of screen that recorded the bullets that hit it; this was done by placing the tips of the bullets in different colored paints. The pilots towing the targets were army privates. They had started in the sergeant flying program but had been court-martialed for an infraction of the rules, but could still fly airplanes.

1944. We flew home to Moore Field in Mission, Texas from gunnery training on the fourth of January. This was a red-letter day for that afternoon I was commissioned as a second lieutenant in the army. The best prize of all was the Silver Wings of a pilot. This was a sign to the whole world that you had the right stuff. The picture below shows me in my new officer's uniform, the "pink" pants, green tunic, and

the fifty-mission hat.

After graduation from cadetship, there was a big house party in Minneapolis, Minnesota. After the party I flew home on Mid-Continent Airlines. The plane took off from Minneapolis and headed to the Sioux Falls, South Dakota. After gaining the cruising altitude, the pilot came out of the flight deck. I was sitting in the front seat and he said go up front. When I arrived on the flight deck, the co-pilot said, "Take over. I have paperwork to do." I sat down at the controls of the Lockheed Electra passenger plane. It was the first time I was ever at the controls of a twin-engine airplane. The co-pilot said I was to maintain the heading and altitude at which we were flying. He also pointed out the

Lockheed XC-35
USAF Museum Photo Archives

beacon at the Sioux Falls airport. After landing in Sioux Falls, a young lady boarded the aircraft. She said it was her first flight and she was afraid to fly at night. I told her I had just flown down from Minneapolis and the weather was perfect. Night flying, I told her, was very smooth and enjoyable. Our next stop was Sioux City, Iowa. Upon landing, I noticed that we had picked up some rime ice on the tail. This is very dangerous as it disrupts the air flow over the wing and you lose lift. This is the airplane I was flying.

We took off from Sioux City and immediately ran into icing conditions. The cockpit door was opened and I could see the instrument panel. What I saw on the instrument panel was scaring me to death. The pilot had both engines at full throttle, the de-icing boots were on, and we were losing altitude at a rapid rate. I was sure we were about to crash. The lady sitting across the aisle said that night flying was really nice and she was enjoying the flight. The pilot gained control at about one hundred feet, and flew all the way to Omaha down the Missouri River.

So too much knowledge can be a bad thing.

After a short visit at home, I went back to Washington, D.C. to visit my sister Betty. While she was at work, I visited the Smithsonian Museum. The Spirit of Saint Louis was there, and it had been lowered for some work. The worker saw me standing there and told me to come in and have a look. It was quite a sight for a new pilot. The cockpit of that famous plane! There is no forward vision, only out the sides. It was a great privilege to have such a rare opportunity. From Washington I took a train to Jacksonville, Florida, where I boarded a local train to Tallahassee for my first duty station at Dale Mabry Field. It was a single-engine pilot depot. From there we were sent to fighter/bomber training, which took place at Waycross, Georgia, flying the P-40 as pictured earlier in this text. We did our ground strafing and bombing in the Okefonokee Swamp, and our aerial gunnery over the Atlantic Ocean. During this period 100-grade octane gasoline became very scarce and we had to fly with 92-grade octane. This created quite a problem and we had a thrill every minute. The airplane did not have the pickup that we were used to and

because of that we had several accidents.

When we arrived in Waycross, the army had to put us up in a hotel because there was no coal to heat the barracks. Such was life during the war.

When we had finished our flight training, we were sitting around when one of our instructors was called to fly to McDill Air Force Base to pick up the classified mail. Four of us got on the airplane and flew to Tampa with our instructors. Before getting back on the airplane, I picked up a sandwich in Base Operations. The only sandwich left was Limburger cheese. I tucked the sandwich under my arm in my flying suit and boarded the airplane. Half way home I pulled out the sandwich and started to unwrap it. I knew what was going to happen. I was going to be jumped and have the sandwich taken away. That was what happened and with the first big bite the grabber was sick out the window of the plane. We all had a good laugh at the expense of the Limburger cheese-eater. Upon our return home, there was a big reception committee with the wing commander and the whole staff. The reason for such a welcome was that the classified mail was still in Tampa. And we were not supposed to fly anymore. So we were back to Florida for our next assignment.

All the pilots who had finished fighter/bomber training met in a theater for further assignment. An officer would read out the needs of different units and asked for volunteers. All of the married pilots chose to go to Alaska where they deemed it would be safer. We volunteered for tactical reconnaissance training for two reasons: The first was that we got thirty days' leave, and second, we would be flying the P-51 Mustang.

I was home for thirty days before reporting to Key Field Meridian, Mississippi, for tactical reconnaissance training. While home on leave, I had the presence of mind to call a friend who was a commercial photographer. This picture is

the last one ever taken of my family.

Who are all these people? Well, standing on the left is Ruth McKenzie Smith; she is the daughter of the woman seated in front of her. Ester Holton McKenzie, wife of Guy

Cameron McKenzie (deceased), brother of R. E. McKenzie Lear, my grandmother. She is seated fourth from the left. Standing next to Ruth is Arthur Graham Sr., husband of Eleanor Lear, daughter of Mrs. Lear. Next is the author's father, Julius Neal Clemmer Sr., and the author. Next on my right is Colina McKenzie Root; she is the daughter of Colin McKenzie, next to her, and then her mother Lina McKenzie. Seated is Ester, then my sister Betty, next is Eleanor Lear Graham, next her sister Emily Lear Weisdorfer. Eleanor and Emily are the daughters of Mrs. Lear, whose third daughter was my mother, Colinette Lear Clemmer. Just below Betty is our grandmother, Laura May Cox Clemmer, who is seated next to Grandfather Joseph Neal Clemmer. Then Grandmother Rhoda Elisabeth McKenzie Lear. Mrs. Lear's brother, Dave, is next. Seated on the floor are Bill Smith Ruth's eldest son, then Dick Graham, Bob Smith, Ann Root, Colina's daughter, then Buddy Smith.

My first flight was on June 9 on a P-40N. It was on the

version of the P-51, Notice the dive flaps in the wings.

Yes, that is me at the controls, and I am very thankful to have such a picture, as very few pilots have such a memento of their flying days. This would be a good place to put in the photo that I took over Mississippi while in training.

You can just see the car on the bridge.

My friend, John Corson, had met a nurse in Florida who was from Birmingham, Alabama. She was home on leave at this time and invited John and me to visit her there. We checked out every way there was to get to Birmingham, but there was no way. Anyway, John and I had to fly that Saturday so we flew to Birmingham twice in our P-51s. That afternoon, in desperation, John went to see the base commander about an airplane, and the commander gave us an L-2 for the trip.

North American P-51D "Mustang"
USAF Museum

fifteenth of June when I flew the P-51 for the first time.

Here we learned to take aerial photos, one of which I will include, adjust artillery, more aerial gunnery, and navigation. While there, I was flying wing for one of the other students when I looked up. I could see his camera so I radioed him to snap a picture of me. Here it is. Only I am flying the A-36, the dive bomber

That saved the day, and we enjoyed some real Southern hospitality. Upon returning, our instructor asked where we had been, as he was looking for us. When we said that we had flown to Birmingham, he was really mad as he couldn't get a plane for a cross-country but his students could.

On the seventeenth of July we flew down to Mobile, Alabama, in Bates Field for aerial gunnery practice over the Gulf of Mexico. All I can remember about that time was strafing a very large Ray by a small island. After five days there, we returned to Key Field to finish our training, which ended on the first of August.

When I talk about "we," I am referring to the officers whom I had trained with since advanced flight training in Texas.

From left standing: Bob Bruce, John Corson, "Pinkie" Eskelson; seated, Harvey Maher, E.J. Kinney III, and the author.

We left Key Field for Savannah, Georgia, where we staged at Hunter Field

From Hunter Field, we went to New York at Fort Hamilton. There we boarded the luxury liner Mauritania (her sister ship, the Lusitania, was sunk during World War I by the Germans) and headed for the war in Europe. The ships sailed south to pick up the Gulf Stream and headed for England. The reason was to follow the fog bank across the North Atlantic. One night north of Ireland, the ship was

You can just see the car on the bridge.

doing hard turns to the left and right, the reason for this was that a tanker had been torpedoed and we were easily seen by the light of the fire. We arrived safely in Liverpool where we took a train south to an airport called Bobbington. From there we flew across the English Channel. When we crossed the French coast, I looked down and saw where the graves were being dug for the American casualties. We landed at A-10, where our outfit had been stationed, on the beach at Normandy, but they had moved out after the fall of Paris and were stationed at Buc Field, which is south of Paris. In fact, the gardens at Versailles were under our landing pattern.

I was assigned to the 109th Tactical Reconnaissance Squadron, 67ᵗʰ TAC. Recon. Gp., IX Tactical Air Command, Ninth Air Force.

The next morning, I got on a truck and went into Paris. I was not the usual tourist, as I wore a steel helmet, carried a .45-caliber handgun, and had my pants tucked into leggings. We had arrived in our outfit the night before too late for dinner, I got up too late for breakfast, but they had sent rations in on the truck. The truck was parked under the Eiffel Tower so it was easy to find. We went to the truck to get something to eat, but the supply officer had sold the rations on the black market.

I flew over Europe for the first time on the eighth of September; it was a flight from Paris to Le Havre and back. I did the navigation out and my wingman was to bring us back. He took off to the north instead of the east so I called him back and headed for Paris. When we arrived over Paris, he spotted the Eiffel Tower and proceeded to buzz it. That afternoon an officer came to my tent and asked if I had buzzed the tower. I replied that I hadn't, and he asked about my wingman and I said, "Yes, he had." The officer told me that my wingman had come home with about fifty feet of antenna; it had cut through his wing, and halfway through the wing strut. If he had crashed, it would have been the loss of the plane that counted, as the pilot was nothing but trouble from then on.

From the left standing, Bob Bruce, John Corson, "Pinkie" Eskelson, seated Harvey Maher, E.J. Kinney III, and me the author.

I flew my first combat mission on the twelfth of September. It was to Luxemburg and we flew for two hours and twenty minutes. All that time I sat on the C0-2 bottle for the inflatable rafts that were in our seat cushions. It was very hard, and very uncomfortable; had I known where I was, I might have bailed out. However, I returned to base safely. About the middle of September, we moved up to Belgium for our new base. We were at that Belgium base until the twenty-second of March 1945.

On October 29, I flew with Major Robinson to a town in Germany called Prum. It seems somebody at higher headquarters knew something they wanted us to look at. I flew another reconnaissance mission on the seventh of November to Prum, Germany, and I can still see the German tanks sitting on flatcars in the railroad yard. We flew to Prum again on the eighteenth of November as higher headquarters was interested in the German buildup. Well, they should have been, for it was where the Battle of the Bulge started.

Shortly after arriving in Belgium, a flight of B-26 bombers had to abort a mission, and it seemed that every plane was on its own to find a safe landing site. Three of these medium bombers spotted our base and decided to land. We only had three thousand feet of grass runway for them, and that was way too short.

Earlier in the day a convoy of trucks carrying 100-grade octane fuel for the airplanes arrived at the base gate. When no one in authority could be found so the M.P. said, "Stack it over there." So a gas dump was located at the southwest corner of the field. Normally, this would not have been a problem. However, when the first B-26 came in, the pilot was instructed to pull up his wheels as soon as he touched down. The pilot chose to make wheels down landing and when he hit the brakes he skidded right into the new gas dump. The crew got out as there was no fire. The second pilot was also told to pull up his wheels, but he did not and also skidded into the gas dump. With that there was a tremendous fire, but that crew got out also. The third pilot pulled his wheels and bellied in, As the plane slid down the runway, the crew were seen running the other way.

Several of us were standing there, watching the show, as the bombs were bursting, sending up exploding ammunition from the machine guns. Then the tail gun in the second plane started firing, sending bullets past us about knee-high. That ended our rubbernecking as we ran to safer grounds.

John Corson met a Monsieur Barrie who invited him to visit at his home, and bring a friend. So one evening John and I started out to find Monsieur's house. We got terribly lost, but a man came up to us and asked if he could be of help. Of course, we had no idea where we were. His mother spoke English she had learned from the Canadians during World War I. She phoned Monsieur Barrie for directions, and took us by streetcar to the right place. The interesting thing about this encounter was that the family had hidden an American bomber crew in their attic until it was safe for them to be moved. The crew did get out safely and had written to the family thanking them for the great kindness that had saved their lives from German capture.

John and I grew very fond of the Barrie family and their kindness. It was all "give" on their part as they asked nothing in return for the many nice things they did for us over the winter of 1944-45.

For example: you cannot imagine what a hot bath is like when you haven't had one in a very long time. Then there were the gourmet meals, with the best wine you ever tasted. For example, one meal I will always remember was during the winter of 1944 when we were served, for the salad course, a ripe tomato stuffed with shrimp. It was canned shrimp that Mr. Barrie had hidden in his wine cellar since the war started in 1939. He thought so much for us that he was willing to share such rare treat with us.

The meals at the Barrie house were nothing like you have ever seen. After each course, someone would get up and entertain. They would sing, recite a poem, play an instrument, or something. We were asked to entertain but there was nothing we could do. John had played the flute in the college band so his mother sent it to him. This left me little choice, and I had to perform too. I went to the music store and there was an ocarina, also called a sweet potato. A fruit flute. So John and I worked on two Christmas carols, as we had been invited for Christmas dinner.

Christmas dinner was to start at noon, so we set up a signaling system to let the family know what was going on. If we had to fly on Christmas day, we would fly low over their house to let them know we were going to combat, upon return we would buzz them again to signal our safe return, and to expect us in an hour or so later. An hour later, I was over their house again heading for combat. Upon my return I buzzed again. My wingman had no idea what was going on

This is a picture of the Barrie family at their front door. Jennie, Madam, Mr., Janet, and a young Dutch girl they had taken in as there was no food in Holland at that time.

with all this low flying.

In retrospect, the Barrie family must have felt badly for us, and were anxious to see if we would return from combat or not. The wait was two hours each time.

John and I managed to get to the Barrie house at 8:00 PM on Christmas night, and we were just in time for dessert. The dessert was a Yule log of chocolate and butter. After the dessert was finished, John and I pulled the hidden instruments out and played our tunes. Now I will be the first to admit they were awful, but it pleased Mr. Barrie greatly that his two American friends would entertain his family at Christmas.

After buzzing the house the first time I flew a mission to Bastogne, which was made famous for not surrendering to the Germans. I spotted more than fifty armored German vehicles in a wooded area. So I called for fighter support, and got a group of P-38s with napalm. I put the group leader and his wingman on my left wing, and my wingman, Chick Childers, on my right and in we flew in and strafed the target. As we pulled off the run, the P-38 leader said he did not see the target. Our standing rule was one run, as they would shoot you down on the second pass, and we were to get home with the intelligence, not fight. So a second pass was necessary. What I did was an old trick from World War I. I flew the formation around until I had the sun in my rear vision mirror, and we came in out of the sun so that the Germans couldn't see us.

On the second strafing run, the group leader saw the target and set up their bombing runs. There was soon a very intense fire that attracted the attention of a squadron of P-47s. So they joined in with five-hundred-pound-high explosive bombs to finish off the job. I called Chick and said, "Let's head for home, there isn't any more we can do here."

I have talked about flying missions and perhaps it is time to explain the types we flew. There were basically three types of missions: artillery adjustment, photographic missions, and visual missions. On a photographic mission, you were assigned an altitude, a direction, and an air speed. These pictures were to be used by the artillery when they captured the ridge over which you flew. This type of mission meant you were a sitting duck as you had to hold your altitude, air speed, and direction, so that the enemy gunners could get a very good aim at your plane. Luckily, I only flew one such mission. I flew several artillery adjustments, and the ones I remember best were as follows.

Late one afternoon, I was sent to adjust artillery. I contacted the unit by radio and called for them to fire for effect. When I said "fire," they would fire one shell and then called "splash" at ten seconds before impact. This gave me an opportunity to turn the airplane up on the wing and watch for the impact. You then radio them whether they were over, under, left or right. This way the artillery could tell what was happening to a shell in flight. When I had finished adjusting for that outfit, another called for help, when I finished with them a third radioed in. When I had finished, a different voice came on the radio saying "thank you," you have adjusted 273 artillery pieces for the night. This meant that all night they could drop shells, at random times and places, to keep the Germans from being able to move troops or equipment.

Another memorable shoot was a counter-battery fire on a German artillery unit that was horse-drawn. The mission was during the Rose Pocket when we had the Germans surrounded, and it was my first experience with proximity-fused shells. Every shell they fired was an airburst, and I thought they were exploding when they hit the trees, but I found later what they really were.

A third artillery shoot was on a bridge that I had zeroed in for a shell to land directly on the bridge. Then a German staff car started for the bridge. As the staff car was approaching the bridge, they called "splash." I expected to get both the bridge and the car, but the car crossed the bridge. It was just at the other side of the bridge when the shell hit the staff car directly. I took some pictures of the scene to send to the artillery unit; there was not a sign anywhere in the picture that there had been a staff car on the road.

The majority of my missions were the visual type such as the missions to Prum, Germany. These missions were to watch the enemy for troop movements of any kind. We would report trucks, trains, marching troops, new gun emplacements, etc. On one such visual missions that I flew, I was briefed to check if there were any bridges across the Rhine River. I flew from Cologne to Koblenz, and the only bridge standing was at Remagen.

The mission board determined who had the next mission. When you returned from a mission, your name was put on the bottom of the board. As each pilot flew, your name was moved up until you reached the top again. On October 10, 1944, my name reached the top three times. Three combat missions in one day! That happened only once, but I have flown two combat missions on six other dates.

While waiting for a call to be briefed for a flight, the pilots sat around the "ready room" and played cards, mostly the games we had learned as kids. A bridge player arrived in the unit and there was no one to play bridge with, so he started giving lessons. Soon every pilot was a bridge player, and the former "rowdy room" became very quiet. As you will see later, playing bridge was to ease my way into making college friends.

I was very lucky to have had an oil painting done of me in 1944 in Belgium. The artist was Archie McClain.

I got the canvas for this portrait while I was in London on flack leave.

Some of my pictures tell a story of the mud we had to fly from. For the non-flying reader, let me explain that an airplane engine is ran on magnetos (small generators), of which there are two. Before taking off, you run the engine up, at the end of the takeoff runway, to near full power to check the magnetos. If you get a drop of 100 rpm on either magneto, you don't fly, unless you are crazy. Anyhow, the mud was so deep at that time that it took nearly full power just to

taxi, so we checked our "Mags" on the way to takeoff.

This photo shows the cold and snow during the winter of 1944-45.

All was not work, there was some time to play too. This is a German motorcycle that was "liberated."

Yes that is me on the cycle.

I mentioned earlier the mission board that told who was next up to fly combat. From November 1944 until April 1945, my name was never off that board, That meant there was never a day, for six months, that I had a single day that I didn't face the fact that combat with a deadly enemy was just a call away.

After my first five combat missions, I received my first Air Medal. As you can see, I was a happy camper.

Before the war was over, I received fourteen more Air Medals, and four Battle Stars. There were five major battles for the liberation of Europe, for which Battle Stars were awarded. It went to those who were in those battles, and as

stated I was in four.

1945. I flew dawn patrol this memorable day, and got shot up pretty badly by the Americans-they had been shot at by the Germans earlier and as their motto goes-"Shoot 'em down and sort 'em out on the ground." Flying through all that flack-anti- aircraft artillery-AAA. The mechanics had to get my plane a new propeller as it had been badly damaged.

It was during this time that I flew the mission to see if there was a bridge still standing over the Rhine River. I reported that there was one at Remagen. That night I was the Group Officer of the day. When I reported in, there was an intelligence officer up on a step ladder looking at the situation map. I asked him what was up and he replied that we had crossed the Rhine. I told him that the only bridge was at Remagen. He found it on the map, but said it was too far south, and I said, "Check my morning report. It is the only place that anyone could cross." The next morning, the news was we had crossed over at Remagen, and you know the rest of the story.

The next base was at Limburg, Germany. We were there until April 11 when we moved to Eswege, Germany, where we remained until the end of the war.

On May 11, I started flying the UC-78, seen next.

I flew this plane to Holland on the day the war ended. We had filed a flight plan to return to Germany, but refilled in the air on our way to Belgium. The next day, we flew back to Eswege and upon entering the traffic pattern there was a German JU-88 also in the pattern. The tower advised me of his presence, and I replied that he only wants to see which way to land. Then the tower advised me that I was being shot at by the JU-88. I took evasive action by heading for the ground, and turning in the side of the JU-88. Our AAA (see above) shot the plane down. However, one gunner had been asleep in his tent when the shooting started. He ran out to his gun and asked, "What was going on?" Someone told him there was a German plane in the pattern. As I flew out from over one of our hangars, the gunner started shooting at us. His guns, Quad fifties and four .50-caliber machine guns were facing in the wrong direction, so he kept shooting until he was shooting over my head. I could see the tracer bullets as he pulled

That is me standing on the wing of our UC-78.

the guns down, then he stopped. Had the guns been pointing the other way, who knows what might have been?

After the war I flew a lot of courier flights for the Group. For a message, I would fly the P-51, for larger loads I used the AT-6, for a big load I flew the UC-78. One courier flight I took was to take an officer to Paris to get a flight home to the States. His bag didn't fit the baggage compartment, so I turned the back seat around to put it behind the seat. It just fit, but we couldn't turn the seat around. So he flew to Paris facing backwards. I stopped to refuel at our old base in Belgium. We had a B-17 Flying Fortress attached to our unit after the war; it was used to take people up to see the war damage. On the same day I was in Belgium, the B-17 brought some of our native Belgian workers back for a visit. John came with them, saw the AT-6, and guessed where I was. We missed connections and John was AWOL. I was the one UC-78 pilot in the unit and it was up to me to get our men back from Belgium. Everybody wanted to be my co-pilot, but I had to save a seat to bring John home, so I turned them all down, and flew the plane

16

solo to Belgium, without a map, I might add.

Here are some pictures taken at the end of the war. My room-mate from Omaha, Spider Hansen, who checked

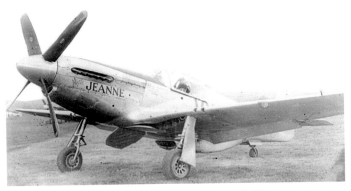

One more picture of me in my P-51.

These are pictures of the damage done to the town of Duren, Germany, during the war.

me out as a twin-engine pilot.

My unit was scheduled to go to Japan from Germany, but those of us who had flown so many missions were allowed to go home. It started with our going to Paris as the first step. There, we were told that we would be there for three days at the most. If our name was not called at noon, we could go to Paris. We stayed at that location for six weeks, thinking each night was the last in Paris.

We finally sailed for home, on a Liberty Ship, landing in Boston many days later. As the deputy commander of the troop train, I went to Fort Leavenworth in Kansas. There I was relieved of active duty.

My cousin, Ruth Smith (in the picture above), took me to lunch at the Omaha Athletic Club after I returned home. Ruth spotted a friend and asked if I minded if she joining us for lunch. Of course, I had no objection. Ruth's friend turned out to be Bess Howard, my first grade teacher. Somehow, she wasn't as big as I had remembered.

Betty and her husband, Carl Tuttle, came to Omaha for a visit; they were on their way to Mexico to visit our father. I

joined them for the trip down, and all the way back to Washington, D.C. I returned to Omaha and was faced with finding a future. The erosion along the Missouri River hit me as I flew to and from Omaha. I decided to study soil conservation, and work for the government. While trying to decide where to go to school, my cousin, Art Graham, called me on the thirtieth of December to tell me that Iowa State College was filling up fast. So the next morning at 4:00 AM, we left for Ames, Iowa. I was still filling out paperwork when Art came back and said we had to go. He wanted to get home for New Year's Eve.

1946. We returned on the second of January, and I went back to filling out the paperwork to enroll. As I was about to finish, the lady said, "You should be in class." So with her directions, off I went, without a notebook, pen or pencil, to my first ever class.

I was playing bridge in the Iowa State College Student Union one day when my partner had to go to class. She handed her cards to a girl to take her place. Well, this girl just sat there and talked. I said, "Did you come here to play bridge or to talk?" This was the start of what has been a fifty-six-year romance; her name was Mary Jane Gray, from Augusta, Georgia. I visited her that summer and we went to the moun-

These pictures are to show what we looked like at that time.

tains of Carolina with her aunt and her stepmother Margaret.

These pictures are from our time in college.

While at Iowa State, I rented a room from Jim Phipps and his mother. This is Jim, his son, and I

On the twenty-eighth of December 1946, Mary Jane and I were married in the Church of the Good Shepherd in Augusta, Georgia.

Our wedding reception was held at the Magnolia Villa. It was ran by the Misses Parkers who were from Kentucky.

This house was on Milledge Road and Walton Way across the street from the church.

1947. In June, Mary Jane graduated from Iowa State. We were living in a converted chicken house, as housing was very difficult to come by. Art Graham, his wife Phyllis, their son Mike, and daughter Judy were there at the same time.

I went to Omaha in the spring and flew with the Reserve from Offutt AFB. They were going to call up reservist to ferry P-51s from Texas to the Northeast. They never called me, but it was fun flying over my home town for the first time. I also landed on the North-South runway, which was closed to make the first SAC museum.

1948. Just a year of work and study. This summer quarter Iowa State College restarted an agricultural trip that had been suspended during the war. The trip started from Ames, Iowa, with two buses, one for the students to ride in, and the other for our supplies. The supply bus went straight through to our next camp site, where we set up our tents and fixed the evening meal. The student bus made several stops during the day. We stopped to see various soil types, visit factories, or ranches and farms of all kinds.

One of our first stops was in Omaha, Nebraska, to take a tour of a very large meat packing plant. The cattle were brought in to the Omaha stockyards by train (hence the term "cattle car"). In the stockyards the animals were sorted out, some went to the slaughterhouse; others went to feed yards to be fattened up before slaughter.

The fat cattle were driven up a ramp to the fourth floor of the packing plant for slaughter. This was done so that the weight of the animals went down the assembly line by gravity and no power was required. As each animal reached a certain point in the process, an act was performed, such as removing a hoof, skinning a certain part, etc. The final act was the making of dog food in the basement of the plant.

The meat was sent out in boxcars as quarters, hind, or front and the final butchering was done at the local level. While we were in Omaha, we also visited the alcohol plant, where alcohol was assessed for taxes at $17.00 a gallon, as it came from the still.

When we reached Wyoming, we visited the Wyoming Hereford Ranch owned at that time by Quaker Oats. The ranch was noted for its many million-dollar bulls. Bulls that have had sired calves worth that amount of money. The ranches' pride and joy was a bull named Prince Domino, which was buried on the ranch with a very fitting large monument to his memory. The Prince was the founder of the Domino line of cattle. He had just won best of show in Chicago, and the ranch turned down a million dollars for him. On the trip home the Prince caught pneumonia and died.

The trip then turned South, seeing the soil types and plants change as we went. We went clear to the Mexican border, which we crossed to have a meal.

Turning north again, we visited the King Ranch, the biggest layout in Texas. I had flown over the ranch during my training at night, and there never was a light for many miles. The ranch started its own breed of cattle to prosper in the Texas climate. It is the Santa Gratuda Breed, which is five-eights short horn and three-eights Indian cattle. They also had race horses, one of which had won the Kentucky Derby.

From there we visited rice farms and cotton plantations before heading north again. The next stop was the limestone country of Kentucky with their horse farms. The one we visited was the Calumet Farm. The barns there were so clean you would never know there were horses living there.

1949. I graduated on the nineteenth of March, and we moved to Augusta. There, on the twenty-third of June, we were blessed with the birth of our first child, Susan Jane Clemmer. During this year I had several short-term jobs. The first was at the Augusta National Golf Club. I worked there in the press tent with Grantland Rice and O. B. Keeler, who were both great sportswriters of the time. My duty was to take the score card from the scoring tent to the press tent. There I would read off the numbers to be recorded on the scoreboard. This is the sad part: On each card were the two signatures of the golfers. All the greats of that time Snead, Hogan, among others. After the scores were posted, I threw the cards away. Today, they would bring big bucks on eBay. The picture below was taken at the Augusta National in 1949. Mary Jane, with her mother, Alta Boyce Gray, and the author.

You should also know that in 1949 the touring golf pros held a golfing clinic on Wednesday afternoons for the club members. I went to the clinic, which I would guess was worth more than you can put on your MasterCard today. The driver demonstration was the best in the business for many years, Sam Snead. Then a demonstration of long irons by another great, Ben Hogan. Mid irons fell to Jimmy Demerit and the short iron pro escapes me. The pros all seemed to be having a great time among themselves as a small gathering watched. Can you guess what that lesson would have cost? For everything else, there is MasterCard.

1950. My job now was to run a dairy. The only thing that I didn't do was milk the cows. I pasteurized the milk, washed and filled the bottles, and delivered them to homes and stores. In addition I was to collect for the service. When no one paid, I found out that the men I was working for didn't own a thing, and that the pasteurizer was about to be taken back, because they owed everybody money. The only good thing about that job was housebreaking the cows. We were milking forty-five cows, and each thought that the barn was their potty. So each milking called for cleaning out of the barn, by hand, for the men who did the milking This took forever and twice a day! So as I was not milking I would run from cow to cow and hold down the tail that kept them from going. When I left the dairy, there was only one cow that had to be cleaned up after, now forty-four cows behaved themselves in the barn. The men who did the milking thought I was the best thing since canned beer.

1951. This year I had the best job ever. I was the herd manager at the Goshen Plantation. At the three-thousand-acre layout owned by Mr. Spear, his son Dick was the overseer, and I was the number-two man. Mary Jane and I had an apartment in the Manor House. The perks were great: free gas for the car, free milk, cream, butter, some vegetables, and I could walk to work. My clothing was simple, jeans, cowboy boots, shirt, and a straw hat. I had a horse to ride to check the cattle herds, of which there were four. We had two breeding herds of cows, and a bull for each herd. A steer herd was raised for market, and a heifer herd was also raised to join the breeding herd when they matured. I had coffee every morning with Dick and a drink at the end of the day. There were several African Americans who worked on the plantation and did all the hard work.

While working for the Spears, I was offered a superb deal to take over a plantation in South Carolina. But it turned out to be a bum deal and we moved back to Augusta.

1952. Our second daughter, Louise Lear, was born on March 19. A second blessing!

I returned to active duty with the U.S. Air Force, and was sent to Germany to join the 603rd Aircraft Control and Warning Squadron. It was based at Giebelstadt, Germany. The base had been Hitler's secret base for testing jet planes, rocket planes, etc. So he had the town taken off the map and may still be off the map up to this day.

During my wait for Mary Jane, I was housed at the Villa Greb in Oxenfurt, Germany. Up the street was the Golden Swan Inn, the barmaid was Gertrude, and everyone knew her. One evening after supper, we had delivered our flight surgeon to his quarters and we saw Gertrude and one of our

This is a self portrait taken in Germany before Mary Jane and the girls arrived.

# — CHAPTER IV —
# The Fourth Decade

1953. Mary Jane, Susan and Louise came to Germany in the spring. Mary Jane and I went to Holland for tulip time.

We had this picture taken for our Christmas card from Germany this year.

Just before Christmas, we welcomed our third bundle of joy. Elizabeth Gray was born on the twentieth of December. Mary Jane's mother arrived on the twenty-first. We had seven for the Christmas dinner on the twenty-fifth. Beth was not counted as having dinner with us.

1954. This summer we went to Paris with Betty and John Dodds. It was a fun trip as Mary Jane and John both tried to speak French but couldn't understand a word, I did all the talking. Here is a picture taken in Paris.

The girls stayed behind with our maid, Barbara

On our way back from Holland, we stopped to see the Barrie family in Jumet, Belgium. Madam had died, the girls were both married, and Grandmer was keeping house. It was an emotional return to the place where I had so many happy memories during such a dark time in history.

John Dodds was our senior controller at the radar site. One day, there was a blip (bogie, enemy, unknown) on the screen next to the East German border, so I scrambled a pair of fighter aircraft to check it out. Soon the "office types" showed up to watch the action. I had the fighters very close to the border when someone poked me in the back, so I turned around to see what they wanted. No one moved so I went back to the scope, and again I was poked in the back, so I turned again with the same result. The blip went away so I took the fighters home. The next Saturday at officers' call, Maj. Jim Williams started talking about officers sitting at the scope and not knowing what to do, and turned around with a questioning face looking for help. So I said "You are talking about me, aren't you?" He said yes. So I asked who poked me in the back when I was controlling the fighters so close to the enemy border. John admitted it

21

was he and said he was pointing at the plotting board where it showed the fighters very close to East Germany. With that explained, I was exonerated.

We went to Garmish for Thanksgiving. We all tried to ski, even Mary Jane.

Here are the skiing Clemmer girls.

The family toured the Linderhof Castle where this picture was taken. Beth walked under the ropes that were to protect the artifacts, so I had to carry her the whole way.

Here is a picture of radio station DL4XR that I built, and talked with ham operators around the world.

A picture taken for Christmas 1954.

Before Mary Jane arrived, we talked by radio almost every day. I became fascinated with the concept of ham radio, and got my radio license in Germany. The call letters were DL4XR. Soon I started to build my own radio station. It drove the family nuts, but it kept me busy nights after work. Here is a picture of radio station DL4XR that I built, and talked with ham operators around the world.

In late January, our unit was moved back from the eastern border. We were housed in Kaiserslautern, but our radar was at Langerkopf on top of a mountain. It was so cold that winter that the diesel fuel froze and shut the unit down.

One night at the Officers Club, someone suggested that we take a Rhine River cruise. That sounded like a great idea at the time, we called the maid and told her we would not be home. Off the whole crowd went to Mannheim, Germany, and got on the boat for Cologne. It was a lovely day and we sat out on the deck watching the beautiful scenery float past.

The idea was that we would have dinner, and spend the night there before returning home. We had the usual steak dinner with wine at the Dom restaurant. It is next door to the great Cologne Cathedral. The cathedral was a beacon for navigation during the war, as it was never bombed. There was not a room to be had any place nearby, so I suggested that we take the train back. We could make berths out of the seats on the train, and get some much needed sleep. We all trouped to the train station. There was a train due soon, great luck. We asked how long a trip it was back to Mannheim, and the clerk said two hours. We were home sooner than we expected.

1955. There were several interesting happenings this year in the aircraft controlling business. The wildest was a lost airplane. I was on duty with my crew when the inspector general and all the brass came in to see the control room. With all that horsepower there, I asked John Dodds to relieve me. The latrine facility was outside the security gate so one had to be relieved to be relieved. With a free pass I went to the snack bar, had a drink and a snack, and returned to the control center. All hell had broken loose in the hunt for a lost airplane. Not any plane but the newest addition to the fighting force, an F-86D. The first fighter with a radar in the nose. It seems the pilot was up for a short ride and was lost by the unit that was to have the plane under control. Everyone was looking for him, and the best advice given was to turn west before he entered hostile territory. The whole episode was a "Chinese Fire Drill." A lot of people got involved that should not have.

The pilot reported that he was low on fuel, then he spotted a hole in the overcast and announced that he was going down. A lot of people said no as he would be easier to spot if he stayed at altitude. However, the pilot was in charge and down he went. He reported that he was over an autobahn, heading west. Everyone guessed he was heading for the airfield at Launstule. He was actually one road south, he ran out of fuel, and bailed out. With that, all the brass made a hasty exit, leaving me to do my job. I had a rescue chopper there in twenty minutes. Now guess who had to face a very hostile accident review board. Right-me! Yes, I was on duty, but I was duly relieved by the senior controller. Upon my return all I had to follow the action was a wall speaker, and had no idea what was going on.

This year my tour of duty was over, and we were to rotate back to the USA. Our return was delayed until August. We had to wait until then as Judith Neal did not arrive until the twenty-third of June. Exactly six years to the day after Susan.

Coming home was a story in itself: We flew, but it took twenty-four hours to get from Germany to New York. We stopped to refuel in Iceland and were told they had run out

of room for us to stay. There was a hurricane coming up the east coast. The pilot decided that he could make it to Labrador so we took off again. After refueling the pilot said he could make a dash for New York. Then I wired (that means that I sent a message) to my sister and my father, who both lived in the city at that time, hoping desperately that someone would meet us at the airport.

They all showed up.

Our first stop was at Betty's house to recover from the trip, and while there Carl, Betty's husband, took this picture.

The second stop was to buy a new car, which I did in Brookline, New York. After our visit with Betty, my dad and his third wife, we were off to Augusta, Georgia. Back home after three years, there was a lot to catch up on. Like old friends Alice and Rocky Bazemore, the Spear family, and many others. Dr. Gray was the happiest to see his daughter and granddaughters home safe. The new polio shots were just out and the good doctor wanted to be sure none of his kin got the dreaded disease. All the girls got their shots right away. When the booster was due, the doctor and Margaret came to Roanoke Rapids, North Carolina, on the train to give the girls the shots for polio. The next visit to Augusta the girls were not too happy to see "Granddaddy" and his black bag.

Dick Spear, the owner of the Goshen Plantation, invited us out for dinner, and while there he asked if I would like to see the cow herd. So we went out to the pasture in his pickup to see the cows. All of the cows stopped as we drove up and looked at the truck. When we got out, the cows that I had worked with went back to grazing while the young ones still watched us. Somehow, after all that time, the old cows knew that I was not a threat.

After we were settled, we were visited by our good friends- the Jacobs. We were their daughters' godparents. This is Charley Jacobs with us and Beth in front of 104 Circle Drive, Roanoke Rapids, North Carolina.

When the new commander arrived to take over the unit, I felt that it was my duty to acquaint him with the local people, which I did. For my efforts he kindly wrote in my Officer's Effectiveness Report that I was a "social climber."

In April, the air force sent me to the Rand Corporation for multiple intercept training. It was to test you to find the breaking point when they overloaded you with fighters and enemy targets. The result was that I got to go to MIT for a school on the SHAGE system.

One day, a local man came to the base and asked the commander if the unit could help with a blood drive. I was assigned the task. It turned out that this was do-or-die for the city to stay in the blood bank. The town either had to meet its quota or they would be dropped, no more blood. So I insulted everyone in town as being blood suckers, parasites, living on other people. To keep this as short as possible, I will just include a picture of me being given a citation by the American Red Cross at its Washington headquarters. The donation drive collected 266 pints of blood that day.

Left to right, our commanding general, the author, General Alfred M. Guenther (ret.), Red Cross president, the mayor of Roanoke Rapids, and our unit commander George T. Milonas.

The United States Air Force was so impressed with my civic involvement that they sent a movie crew to film a reenactment of the blood drive.

The radar career field was starting to wear very thin, and I started to look for greener fields. The one I chose was the missile school. My commander and my new boss both approved my application for training. Then a real stroke of luck for me. The Air Defense Command sent out a "secret" message saying that qualified controllers could apply for another career field. My application was at headquarters, so I was ahead of the game. I called the training officer and told him to quote the "secret" message when he forwarded my paperwork. Soon my orders came back for me to attend missile school at Denver, Colorado.

In June, we packed up and left for Denver. The first half of the school was all about electronics. We studied AC-DC electricity, vacuum tubes, etc. Class was from 6:00 AM until noon, and homework took most of the afternoon. The last half of the training was on the missile, so there was no homework.

Washington, DC May 23, 1957

To Captain Neal Clemmer, with deep gratitude for the outstanding assistance you have given the American Red Cross Alfred M. Guenther

Left to right, our commanding General, the author, General (ret.) Alfred M. Guenther, Red Cross Pres. the Mayor of Roanoke Rapids, and our unit commander George T. Milonas.

1956. My next duty assignment was Roanoke Rapids, North Carolina. Not the best of places to be stationed, but we did have good friends and neighbors. I brought home from Augusta a huge antenna tower and a six-bay TV antenna. This allowed us to bring in the Norfolk, Virginia, television programs, the best of which was the Mickey Mouse Club. Every afternoon our living room was filled with all the children in the neighborhood watching their favorite show.

On our first night in Roanoke Rapids, we met the mayor, later the local state senator, and other luminaries in the city.

Before Christmas, there was an item in the Denver paper telling where to go to cut your own tree. On Sunday, we headed out to find the perfect tree, so did everyone else in Denver. At last the girls and I found the right one. I got down and started to saw the tree down, half of it fell over, and the other half was still standing. We had chosen two trees growing as one. I took both halves home and put one half outside the bay window, the matching half inside, and decorated both halves. Most of the passing cars stopped to look, as it appeared as if we didn't have a front window.

1958. School ended and we awaited our orders. After several false starts I was ordered to Camp Cook, California. The orders said about training before shipment overseas. I reported in and was assigned to the 392d Missile Training Squadron. I started home, but remembered that my orders said something else, so I went back to check. Turned out they needed people to stay there too, so began the next seven years of my career.

There was no place to stay as the air force had flooded the area with people. We were lucky to find a house for sale in Lompoc, California. The bank put in for its very first Federal Housing Administration loan for me. The patio was still dirt. We were preparing to go to church.

The first mission of the 392nd was to train the United Kingdom Royal Air Force to use the Thor missile. Of course, we had to be trained first so the air force sent us to Tucson, Arizona, in the summer for training.

1959. The next program was the RAF would receive a new missile from the factory, and ship the oldest one back to the U.S. for launching. The missiles were flown in C-124 aircraft. Someone from our unit went with the missile to England, a big boondoggle. I was always the next to go, and am still waiting for my turn.

1960. Our unit had started a small school called Ballistic Missile Staff Familiarization. General Wade, the commanding general at Vandenberg AFB, mentioned the school at a commanders' meeting at the SAC (Strategic Air Command). General Power, CINSAC, is reported to have gotten up and said everyone present will attend that school. Pictured below is one of such classes that was ran by the author, standing far left.

I was called to General Wade's office upon his return.

Here is a picture taken in the back yard of our house just after we moved in.

1959. Christmas was a big success this year, Santa came through with the right stuff, as the picture shows.

The school was transformed that day from the one-story building, seen in the back of the picture, to a full-blown theater building. The school now had the backing of the general, and instead of getting a second lieutenant, we now got field- grade lecturers for our classes. Lt. General Sweeney, commander of the Eighth Air Force at Westover AFB in Massachusetts, said it would cost too much to send all his people to California. Instead, he sent his KC-135 tanker to take the school to him. Guess who got the job of putting that act together to go on the road? I had to housemother some twenty officers, reminding them to take their raincoats, etc. After arriving, there were the usual problems. One officer was sure that his trousers were under his blouse; they weren't. It not only rained while we were there; a hurricane came through and sure as shooting some of the officers had not packed a raincoat.

Someone talked to the club officer about taking home some lobsters. Soon everyone wanted lobsters to take home. I took names, collected money, and ordered the lobsters to be delivered to the plane. As it turned out I had more lobsters than I had orders for so the extra lobsters were my pay for running a great road show.

BALLISTIC MISSILE STAFF FAMILIARIZATION
COURSE 60-17    12 AUGUST 1960
Vandenberg AFB    California

Mary Jane's mother, "Botie," came for Christmas, which was a tradition by now. So in the spring she started to make plans to return to Augusta. Mary Jane had a better idea: She would drive Botie home with the girls for a visit with the family. So off they went just before school was out. By the time they reached the front gate, the rumors began to fly- she had left me- but why? They had a lot of wrong answers that got back to me, in hopes of some juicy details, but there were none. They are on the front porch of Magnolia Villa.

1961. Botie had a sister in Salinas, California-Aunt Mary. She had married a native Californian, and they had two boys, Glen and Ernest. By the time we arrived in California, the families had grown to include several grandchildren. We visited

them the first time while we were seeking shelter as we had no place near the base to live.

Glen Sevier and I were fishing all day in the surf with no results. Then just after sundown I landed this fish. The season opened the next day.

1962. I built a travel trailer this year so we wouldn't have to stay in motels. It was a great invention with a roof that rose up, four bunks in the back for the girls, a hide-a-bed in the front for the adults. We took it to the World's Fair in Seattle, Washington. Bill, Mary Jane's brother, was there, and Dr. Gray and Margaret came from Augusta. It was quite a time as Bill's wife, Betty, gave birth to their second child, Amy, while we were all there.

This is how the family looked that spring in Augusta.

Picture of our families eating salmon that I had caught the night before.

# — CHAPTER V —
# The Fifth Decade

1963. Things were slow with the Thor program at this time so I was working with the training of the Minuteman program. One morning, while working at my desk, the phone rang and the caller said, "Congratulations." I had no idea what he was talking about; it seems that my name was on the list for promotion to major. What a wonderful piece of news.

I'm sure we were ready for church, probably for Easter.

While at Vandenberg, I was very active in the Episcopal

This picture is taken in front of our quarters at Vandenberg AFB.

Church. The church sat on a lot just one block from the main street of Lompoc, California. The property was going up rapidly in value as the town grew. So the church was sold for a filling station. A new church was built in a walnut grove just north of town. All during this time I was serving on the vestry. When the new church was built, I was the senior warden, and we were having problems with the minister. I led a delegation to Los Angeles to see the bishop and tell him about our problems, seeing how the bishop never came to our church. We asked the bishop to keep our trip to himself as the minister was having mental problems, and this would only make things worse. Well, the bishop, being a good Christian man, called the minister at once and told him everything about our trip to see him. We were then told that to get a new person in the church we would have to give more money to the diocese. This and some other un-Christian church matters drove me from the church.

The air force had a program to use the Blue Star missile. It was a solid propellant rocket with three stages, and was spin-stabilized. As you will see in the picture, it was a rail-fired rocket. The payload was a radio that was programmed

to give the "Go" code to launch the Strategic Air Command fleet of planes and missiles in case of war.

The special building in the picture had a hydraulic roof that opened for the missile to fire. Also the rear wall was hinged to absorb the blast of the engine. I was chosen to be the launch officer for this program and as I recall I was the only air force person on the project. All the other personnel were civilians. The missile was hung on the rail in preparation for launch, all tests were ran and on the appointed day and hour I turned the key. The roof opened, the missile rose on the rail and "bingo" the missile was on its way. After clearing the roof the spin rockets fired, a perfect launch. However, the radio failed to work. The rear wall opened but was blown off by the blast. The building was rebuilt, another rocket was hung on the rail and we were set for launch the next morning, all systems go. About 4:00 P.M. I got word that the program was scrubbed-there would be no second launch. So that missile is in front of the SAC Museum with a Thor and the Atlas, the first two I have launched.

1964. Things picked up rapidly in the Thor business with a new mission. An all "blue suit" (air force) team were to launch satellites. From our launch pads the missile could go due south and not pass over land until it reached the Antarctic. This put the satellites in a sun-synchronous polar orbit. Meaning that it was over Saigon every day at noon.

This new program needed a new countdown manual. That is a checklist for launching the missile. The 4000th Group commander came to the blockhouse and told us that he had just come from the Douglas Aircraft Co. They wanted $70,000 to write the manual. "Tex" Ritter and I sat down at once and wrote the manual for the commander. No charge, I had been counting that weapon system down for many years. I no longer have the picture of our "hangar queen" (the term used for aircraft that spent more time in repair than on the flight line), a missile we used in the RAF program. On the back of that picture I had listed all the countdowns on that one missile and it ran into the hundreds. After a launch by the Royal Air Force, we would rebuild the launch pad, and to check it out we started with "dry counts" and no propellants were used. Then a wet countdown was conducted to check the fuel lines; if successful, a countdown with the liquid oxygen was run. With those operations completed, we would run a "dual propellant" count using both oxygen and fuel. So I had a lot of practice doing that job.

1965. We had our first successful satellite launch on the eighteenth of January. I was the launch control officer for this first-ever event. I turned the key that started the launch sequence.

This is the first missile as it stood on
the launch pad ready for launching.

There was a second launch shortly after the first that did the same thing, but there was no recording equipment on the satellite. The weather data collected was sent real time to Saigon. For this launch, I was the launch director, and I had the full responsibility for the whole program. That meant that it was me who counted down from ten to liftoff.

This plaque was given to me by the Douglas Aircraft Co.
It's supposed to be the original key.

This is the missile as it stood on the pad before launch.

28

At my request, I was transferred to Omaha as training officer for the 4000th Support Group.

1966. I was back in my home town for the first time since 1942. There were many family gatherings with relatives from both sides. My first cousin, Darrel Clemmer, and his wife Fran were with us on Thanksgiving, and we went to their house for Christmas for many years. This is the only picture I have of Darrel. He was wounded in Iwo Jima.

1967. Unlike the promotion to major, I was well aware of the upcoming promotion list for lieutenant colonel. There were eight majors in our outfit, all of whom were eligible to be promoted for the first time. For weeks we tried to figure out the odds on who would be named on the

1968. One late Friday afternoon, our computer expert came into the operations office to tell us that SAC Headquarters wanted our computer needs for the next ten years. My boss loved it, and now he could call us all in for a Saturday meeting. This was to impress the commander that he was a hardworking officer. So no golf, and I was there as required. What SAC was looking for was the users' need for what are now known as work stations. However, at that time they were just called CRTs, short for cathode ray tubes.

A CRT is now known as a computer monitor. Well, the meeting dragged on and at long last the boss had to ask, "What is a CRT?" Well, Bob Graham had been in to see me a few days earlier and left a booklet on the CRTs that his company was making. To answer the boss's question, I went into my desk and threw the booklet about the CRTs on his desk. He was mad, humiliated, and shown up all at once by his assistant, so the meeting didn't last much longer.

About this time it became apparent that a computer could be used to control the satellites in orbit. It had been done manually since the first one went up. There is a lot that to be done to keep a satellite working in space, and all the

list. On the day of announcement the commander was telling first one major then another to be at the morning staff meeting. At the very last second, he told me to be there also. I wondered why he had asked me when so many other majors were there already. To my great relief, I was promoted that very day! I put on the silver leafs, even found a colonel's hat with the lightning on the bill. It was a great day!

calculations had to be checked over and over. Requests were made to IBM, NCR, HP, and others None of them wanted to build a small computer. So a second lieutenant in our outfit offered to build a small computer, write the software, and prove that it would work. Just buy the parts. They did, he did, and the computer took over. This lieutenant later became my son-in-law, Allan Dodge.

1969. I completed my twenty years of active duty this year, and went into retirement. These are official photos taken over the years.

There were no more opportunities to be awarded medals, so this is a good place to display the ones that I earned over the twenty-seven years of service.

1970. We opened an employment agency this year. It was a Snelling & Snelling franchise. It looked like the ideal job for retirement. The company was going to have computers in every office nationwide. This was to give us coverage everywhere anyone wanted to work. Well, the computer never came, the State of Nebraska opened a state employment office (free service), and the air force raised the pay for everyone. The combination killed the business within a couple of years. Being in business, I joined the Chamber of Commerce and the Optimist Club.

1971. This year I was chosen as the outstanding member of the Chamber. We had started an annual celebration about the history of Bellevue, Nebraska, and the SAC. Arrows to Aerospace.

The social event of the year was the marriage of Susan to Allan Dodge. (See 1968.)

This happy group picture below was taken at Susan's wedding. Dr. Gray was with the four Clemmer girls whom he enjoyed.

1972. I was elected to the board of the Chamber and became a director.

Capt.

Major

Lt. Col.

These are official photos taken over the years.

There were no more opportunities to be awarded medals, so this is a good place to display the ones that I earned over the 27 years of service.

This happy group picture was taken at Susan's wedding.
Dr Gray was with the four Clemmer girls which he enjoyed.

# CHAPTER VI

# The Sixth Decade

1973. This year I was elected president of the Chamber of Commerce and the Optimist Club of Bellevue, Nebraska.

My cousin Darrel and I would enjoy telling stories about our parents' dog. The Clemmer family had a dog that had many talents when they lived in western Iowa. The way our grandfather Clemmer told the story, the dog was the best watchdog ever. Our uncle Bob said that the dog knew what you were going to hunt when you walked out the door. My dad said the dog was the best bird dog ever, Uncle Ray said he was a rabbit dog. So Darrel and I named this famous dog "Dewey the Wonder Dog." With each telling, the dog got better and better. So here is a portrait of the wonder dog.

We are not sure just who "Dewey" had sat with, but the odds are that it was Raymond, not my dad.

1974. Selling real estate was not my thing. So I looked into other fields.

At this time Mary Jane was the editor of the Bellevue Leader, one of the ten newspapers printed by the Sun Newspaper Co.

The Sun did an exposé of a sacred cow-Boys' Town. It seemed that there was a boiler work sending out letters implying that a boy might not have a Christmas if the recipient didn't send money. As it turned out, each resident of "Boys' Town" was very rich indeed. They had a portfolio on Wall Street that was tremendous. For the work done by the Sun people, they won the Pulitzer Prize. To celebrate the occasion, there was a party to which all the editors and their spouses were invited. After the main party, we were invited to the owner's house for drinks. This is how I met Warren Buffet who owned the newspapers at that time.

1975. The idea of a golf course work looked like a combination of interests. After all, I am a graduate agronomist.

1976. The Buccaneer Bay golf course had an opening for a worker, and I took the job. I learned to mow greens, fairways, and a lot of other related tasks. For no pay at the time. Later I went to work at Forest Hills for Joe Dennis. Continued my golf course education. Built the back nine holes, and installed the irrigation system with its computer.

1976. This winter I learned to plow the snow with a Jeep, and repair golf course equipment in the off-season.

1977. Jeffery Neal Dodge was our first grandchild.

1978. We moved to Bella Vista, Arkansas, where I took the job as golf course superintendent.

There was a lot to do as the courses had been let go with little or no real work being done. Then there were two nine-hole courses to finish, and soon there were two new courses to build. It was a tough job trying to correct the errors of the past, and fight "city hall" at every turn. It took time but I did win in the end. Upon arriving in Bella Vista, Mary Jane went into Bentonville to see if the local paper could use another reporter.

The answer was a big YES! The paper was going to a daily paper the next day. At this time, the Benton County Democrat, a weekly, was owned by Sam Walton. So Mary Jane had many talks with him. She also was the only reporter to cover the annual stockholders meetings. That is until "Sam" and "Wal-Mart" were discovered by the money people in New York. Years later, in Sam's original store on the square in Bentonville, Arkansas, there was a full wall of stories about Wal-Mart that had been printed in the paper, and everyone had the byline of Mary Jane Clemmer.

We were at many social functions during this time where "Sam" and his wife Helen were also guests.

1979. The Dodges came for a visit and we rented a pontoon boat for a trip on the lake. Here is Jeff at the wheel.

Shortly after arriving in Bella Vista, there was a Turf Grass meeting in Little Rock. The featured speaker for the next morning (Saturday) was the governor of Arkansas. At 8:00 AM sharp, Bill Clinton took the stage. He gave a great speech on the environment and how we golf course superintendents were doing our part. I knew then that Bill Clinton was going beyond being the governor of a poor state.

1980. Maggan Kitten and Emily Coker were born this year.

1981. Julie Dodge was born this year. I started to fly again. This time in Cessnas. My father came to visit so here is a picture of four generations of our family.

Louise said this picture is of her and Emily. The general manager of Bella Vista gave us an all-expense vacation to Hawaii as a bonus for the good work I had done. Here we are enjoying the sunshine in Hawaii.

1982. McKenzie Kitten was born this year. The golf foursome at Bella Vista took a cruise offered by our bank. We flew to Miami and boarded a Carnival Fun ship; this was for the Captain's party.

# CHAPTER VII

# The Seventh Decade

1983. Marty and Bob Gorham, friends from the air force days in Bellevue, came to visit. On Sunday, Mary Jane had an open house to cover for the paper. She called to see if we could bring our friends, as the open house was on a very large farm that produced eggs by the million. It is a sight to see-three houses of caged chickens laying eggs. The eggs roll down onto a belt that brings them to the processing building. Their feed passes by on a belt in front of the cages, and each has a supply of water. The droppings that fall through the wire bottom of the cage are scooped to the end of the building where they become fertilizer. We arrived at the open house and at the head of the receiving line was the guest of honor. He greeted Mary Jane and said, "These must be your guests from New Hampshire." They were stunned to meet the governor of Arkansas, Bill Clinton.

We managed to get the family to Bella Vista, Arkansas, for a family reunion. Again, I had the presence of mind to call a commercial photographer to get family pictures. They got a picture of each family, and all the combinations.

1984.  Steffanie Harold was born this year. We went to Iowa for Thanksgiving.

1985.  In June of this year, Dr. J. D Gray, father of Mary Jane, died.

In October we lost Mary Jane's mother "Botie."

1986.  This is at the dedication of the Rose Garden in memory of Doctor J. D. Gray.

Beth is watching me take a picture of Stefanie

1987.  Hannah Harold was born this year. We took the whole family on a cruise this year, and this is how we looked.

1988.  We flew from Colorado to Boston, Massachusetts, to visit with the Gorhams who were living in New Hampshire, near a lake.  Here is what we looked like then.  When we were in Colorado, we went to the Yellowstone Park.  This is the year of the great fires in the park.

While there, I fished in all the famous rivers: the Madison, Fire Hole, and the Yellowstone.  Here is a picture of me fishing in the Yellowstone River.

1989. At the Masters in full dress.

1990. Jillian Harold was born on July 5 just as her aunt Judy was flying home to Des Moines. We took Betty to see our father in Port Charlotte, Florida. Seen here with his fourth wife, Amanda.

1991. We rented a villa at Seven Springs for three months in the winter. The place was small but we belonged to the club for golf, and dining, among other activities This started the lure to spend the winter in a warm climate.

1992. This winter we rented a two-bedroom villa and the Walkers came from Bellevue to visit.

# — CHAPTER VIII —
# The Eighth Decade

1993. Virginia Abbott was with her family in Naples, Italy. Her daughter and her husband were in the navy at that time. We were invited to visit them, and off we flew to Rome. It was a grand visit. They took us to all the sights, the Isle of Capri, the Amalfi Coast, Herculaneum, everywhere.

1994. After reading the book on Provence, we received a Saga tour entitled "Gastronomy of Provence." It turned out to be one of the best trips we ever took. Two weeks of classes in the morning, and afternoon field trips. We even got to Florence, Italy, over the weekend. This picture shows me chopping an onion for the chief. He fixed a whole meal for us at cooking school. He also did a class on chocolate.

This was at lunch on the Isle of Capri.

1995. We had discovered Alaska and went there four times. The fishing is just great, and the scenery is even better.

Virginia took this next picture as we were leaving the Naples railroad station for Rome. Upon leaving, Virginia gave us a copy of Peter Mayle's book A Year in Provence. That set up our next trip to France.

1996. There was a big celebration for our fiftieth wedding anniversary. Everyone was there at the Colony Cove clubhouse.

1997. Louise had a flat in London so we flew over for two weeks. While there, we went to Paris on the train. The Chunnel, you know. Had a great time with Emily and Louise. We took a tour to the Dells to the "James Harriot" country. This is an example of the miles and miles of rock walls that cover the countryside.

1998. The Colony Cove Golf League members were all Scotch drinkers, or at least we all wore Dewars shirts and hats.

From left: Warren Hunt, Jimmie Bottle, Paul Hanisko, Jimmie Rotatori, the author, and Fred Urda.

On October 16, I got my first and only hole-in-one on the par three 6th at River Ridge. ( See page 79 )

1999. Don and Betty Nielsen came from Bella Vista to visit. Don was in my graduating class at North High in Omaha. He took this picture of us at Honey Moon Island.

The golf group from Colony Cove went to see Green, New York. There are several couples here that come from that town and they are always talking about the place. We had a great time, and were able to take on a tour of the Canadian Maritime at the same time.

I do not know when this picture was taken, but the party started in 1999, on New Year's Eve.

The Harold family welcoming the new millennium, Hannah, Jillian, Ernie, Beth, and Stef.

2000. We received a flyer from USAA about a cruise that was half price. Mary Jane and I could go for just $5,000. It was too good to pass up, so we sent in a down payment, even though the trip was not until 2001. So we had a year to plan, and that was what we did.

2001. The trip started in Copenhagen, Denmark, aboard the Orient Lines ship, Marco Polo. We were to visit twenty cities in fourteen countries over a thirty-day cruise. Here is the schedule.

# GREAT CITIES OF EUROPE
# • MARCO POLO •

| DAY | PORT | ARRIVE | DEPART |
|---|---|---|---|
| 09/01/01 | Depart USA | | |
| 09/02/01 | Arrive Copenhagen (Transfer to Marco Polo) | | |
| 09/02/01 | Copenhagen | Embark | Overnight |
| 09/03/01 | Copenhagen | | 07:00 pm |
| 09/04/01 | Cruise Baltic Sea | | |
| 09/05/01 | Tallian, Estonia | 07:00 am | 06:00 pm |
| 09/06/01 | St. Petersburg. Russia | 06:00 am | Overnight |
| 09/07/01 | St. Petersburg, Russia | | 08:00 pm |
| 09/08/01 | Helsinki, Finland | 08:00 am | 06:00 pm |
| 09/09/01 | Stockholm, Sweden | 07:00 am | 04:00 pm |
| 09/10/01 | Cruise Baltic Sea | | |
| 09/11/01 | Warnemunde, Germany (Berlin) 06:00 am | | 11:00 pm |
| 09/12/01 | Kiel Canal | Daytime Transit | |
| 09/13/01 | Amsterdam, Holland | 08:00 am | 07:00 pm |
| 09/14/01 | Dover, England | 07:00 am | 06:00 pm |
| 09/15/01 | Le Havre, France | 06:00 am | 10:00 pm |
| 09/16/01 | St. Malo, France | 08:00 am | 6:00 pm |
| 09/17/01 | Cruise Bay of Biscay | | |
| 09/18/01 | La Rochelle, France | 07:00 am | 10:00 pm |
| 09/19/01 | Cruise the Atlantic & Bay of Biscay | | |
| 09/20/01 | Porto. Portugal | 08:00 am | 06:00 pm |
| 09/21/01 | Lisbon, Portugal | 08:00 am | 06:00 pm |
| 09/22/01 | Cadiz, Spain | 08:00 am | 06:00 pm |
| 09/23/01 | Casablanca, Morocco | 08:00 am | 06:00 pm |
| 09/24/01 | Tangier, Morocco  Gibraltar | 07:00 am  02:00 pm | 12:00 pm  07:00 pm |
| 09/25/01 | Cruise the Mediterranean | | |
| 09/26/01 | Palma de Mallorca, Spain | 08:00 am | 02:00 pm |
| 09/27/01 | Cannes, France | 12:00 pm | 06:00 pm |
| 09/28/01 | Civitavecchia, Italy | Disemabrk | |
| 09/28/01 | Rome (Sightseeing; transfer to hotel) | | |
| 09/28/01 | Rome (Day at Leisure) | | |
| 09/30/01 | Fly Rome/USA | | |

The trip started off well as we flew business class to Copenhagen. We arrived early in the morning, but could not get on the boat until afternoon. The hotel where we were spending the day had a room to rent so we were able to get some much needed sleep. As we boarded the ship this picture was taken.

The highlight of the trip was the optional trip to Moscow. Flying Aeroflot from St. Petersburg was an adventure in itself. The Kremlin is beyond words; it is full of gold, furs, art, and more.

It was on the railroad trip back to the ship from a day in Berlin that we got the news of the day-September 11. On the ship we had CNN and everyone was stunned! After that our trip was altered, and we didn't get to Morocco as planned.

At our stop in Holland, we went to Zaanse Schans where this picture was taken.

We were in Cambridge, England, at the cathedral for the Friday memorial for the victims of the bombing. The next day we were in Normandy, France, which was a very emotional visit.

The following day, we could not use the tenders to get to St. Malo as it was too rough. I hated to miss this stop.

We did have a great day in La Rochelle, France. We saw Porto, Cadiz, and Lisbon in Portugal, and Barcelona in Spain.

The most interesting stop was the island of Palma de Mallorca. This picture was taken there.

In the mail, we got an advertisement for a river cruise. Starting with three days in Nice, France, a week on the Rhone River, and three days in Paris. We just couldn't pass that up so off we went. It was another great trip and the last day we toured the Chateau country. This was our river ship.

VIKING BURGUNDY

EXPLORING EUROPE IN COMFORT

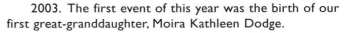

VIKING RIVER CRUISES

2003. The first event of this year was the birth of our first great-granddaughter, Moira Kathleen Dodge.

2002. No trips this year; we had had enough for a while. So on the Fourth of July we went to Augusta to see Margaret Gray. While there, we went to Athens, Georgia, to see Betty Gray as Grace and Ben were there with Vivian too. We had booked a vacation in the North Carolina Mountains for a few days of cool weather. We were staying at the High Hampton Inn. When we arrived, it was hotter than Florida. No air-conditioning, no elevator, no food service (buffet), and I had to wear a suit every night for dinner. Bad deal, but I did catch some fish.

Earlier that year we downsized our transport from a van to a PT Cruiser.

The next event was my eightieth birthday. All the girls were here for a great time. Thank God I got a picture before they left.

# Annex A
# Family History

In order to put a face on the family history above I will include some family pictures that otherwise might be lost. This is a picture of the man who told these stories earlier (see page 49).  Dr. Joseph Neal Clemmer. He was a surgeon in the War Between the States.

On page seven (VII) it tells of Mary Louise Clemmer marrying George Brooks. They had a reunion about the year 1916. Seated in the center of the picture are George, and Mary Louise, Eila Brooks Butterworth is on her grandfather's lap. My Father is the tall kid on the left.

This is my grandmother Laura May Cox Clemmer,
and her three sons. Robert Glen, Raymond Earl,
and Julius Neal my father.

I have no photos of grandfather Clemmer.

This is Charles Henry Lear, Rhoda Elizabeth McKenzie Lear
and their daughter Colinette Lear Clemmer, my Mother.

This picture is of my McKenzie ancestors, seated is George McKenzie, standing on the right is his son George Jr., on the right is George Jr.s' daughter Elizabeth, my grandmother. In front of grandmother is my mother, Eleanor is the tall one, and Emily is on the other side of her grandfather.

No family book would be complete without the grandchildren. From the left our oldest, Jeffery Neal Dodge, his sister Julie Diane Dodge. Then Hannah Harold, Emily Coker, Maggan Kitten, Stefanie Harold, Jillian Harold, then McKenzie Kitten.

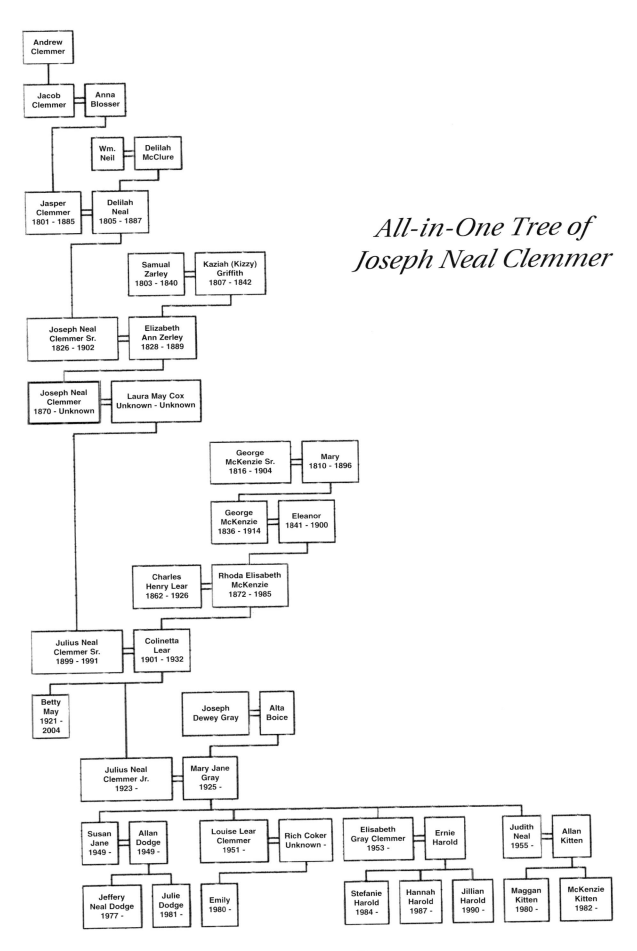

*All-in-One Tree of*
*Joseph Neal Clemmer*

# Ancestors of Julius Neal Clemmer Jr.

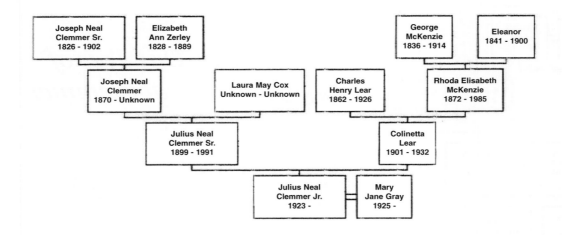

# Descendants of Julius Neal Clemmer Jr.

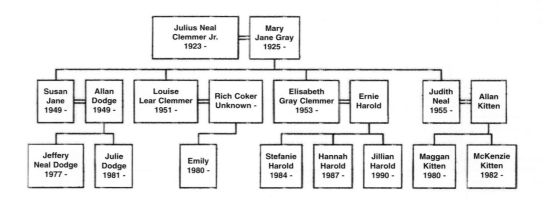

A biographic history of the Clemmer family.
Written by Dr Joseph Neal Clemmer Clarksville Iowa 1900.

The facts I am about to relate were givencto me by my Grandfather Jacob Clemmer - when I
was a small boy - living near Fairchance Furnace Fayette Co Pennsylvania. I was
born Aug 22" 1826.

Our family was originally French - and the name was Klammar' - but it was changed to
Clemmer - giving it an English termination. Our ancestors were descenters from
the Catholic church - Huguenots..In the latter part of the 15" century, the King
of France conceived the idea of bringing all his subjects into the Catholic faith
and in accordance to the custom of the time, an appeal to arms was the outcome.
    The Huguenots and others armed and resisted.

They lived in the mountainous districts of France and were a hardy and thrifty people -
peaceable and loyal to the King in political matters, but when it came to dictating
to them in what they should believe in ecclesiastical matters, that was a different
thing, and a war of unusual violence was the result. After the French had met with
a number of reverses and heavy losses, the King decided,to at least for the present,
conclude an armistice and proclaim peace.

Now comes one of the most damnable pieces of treachery that blackens the pages of history -
namely - the Massacre of what is known in history, as that of Saint Bartholemew's
Eve - an account of which you can find in any reliable history.
    The leading men of the Clemmer family lost their lives in that terrible massacre,
to relate the particulars of which, would take more time and labor than I feel
would be profitable.

Immediately after the massacre, the French government forbid any one leaving the country.
    The priests came with the cross and said "Bow to this" - the soldiers followed
with the sword, and on refusal, the word was "Take this" - and that meant death.

There were three familys - Clemmer Naphf and Blosser - that lived in the same valley and
were great friends. They united and made a strike for liberty - cut their way thro'
the cordon of French soldiers and made their way, or rather escape, into Prussia
and Switzerland. Our folks into Switzerland - settled in Zurah and there the name
was changed from Klammar' to Clemmer. What authority there was in changing the
name I am not able to say.

My great-grandfather (Andrew Clemmer' I believe, came to America when but a young man with
the Blossers and Naphfs. He married a Naphf and settled in the town of York in York
Co Pa. He was a blacksmith by trade, but when the Revolution broke out, he closed
his shop, joined Washington's army and served to the close of the contest - but did
not live long after the war.

Now as to the part my great granmother took in gaining our freedom - she spun the wool, wove
the cloth and made her husband his first uniform - and did so every year he was gone.
    She and her two boys cultivated a small patch of ground - rented the shop - and
from the vegetables they raised, and what the boys earned at small jobs, they
managed to live reasonably well for them.

The two boys - Andrew and Jacob - Andrew was twelve and Jacob ten at the breaking out of the
war. Andrew was a stay-at-home, but Jacob spent most of his time in the British
army - selling doughnuts to the soldiers and picking up any news he could carry to
Washington. I have heard him say that he was but thirteen years old when he first
commenced to spy. He carried on fot two years before the British suspected him and
had him arrested. When he was in the army he could not talk English - and when
they took him before : n officer, all he could say was "Mix for stay" - which meant
he could not understand.

Finally they got an interpreter who was an officer. He asked him a great many questions about Washington, but he knew nothing about him. He then told him to leave the camp and if he ever came back he would have him shot. He would laugh when telling it and say he felt rather streaked. He reported it to Gen'l Washington and he told him not to go any more. He asked for a gun - the Gen'l got one and gave it to him,,and he took his place by the side of his father in the ranks.

He was then sixteen years old and served to the close of the war. He was in the siege of Yorktown and in the charge which compelled Cornwallace to surrender,giving us our independence. He seemed never to weary of telling of that event, and it is not to be wondered at, for it was one of the greatest events in the history of our country - equal to the surrender at Appomatox.

When Jacob grew to manhood he married Anna Blosser. They loaded their household goods on two pack horses, and with others, took the trail across the Alleghanies for what was then known only as the great backwoods - now western Pa and West Virginia. He built his cabin near the banks of the Monongehela river - took his gun on his shoulder and with a hatchet (then called a tomahawk) marked out what land he thought he would need - drove the Indians. away and the government gave him a deed.

It was a long struggle between the early settlers and the Indians; but "poor Lo" has had to go. I could relate many of his adventures with the Indians -but will tell only a small part as I remember now clearly after so many years.

When he landed in the western country they took up their quarters in Fort Swerengen - this they had to do on account of the Indians. All the families in the neighborhood had to do this. The Indians never molested them in the winter - they would chop down the timber, clearing up the land where they intended to build their house, and when it was dry enough, it was set afire and burned.

The men generally had all they could do to watch the Indians. Scouts were constantly on the watch and if they discovered a trail - the alarm was given and every thing was put in order. An armed body of men at once took the trail and a regular game of hide and seek would take place. The whites were as good at scouting as the Indians and when they met it was a fight to the death.

The whites,,being better armed than the Indians, were too much for them - and what was strange - the Indians always came encumbered with their wives and children, but the women had all the work to do. If an Indian kille' a deer, he let it lay and sent his squaw to take care of it. He was too much of a man to do anything of that kind.

A band of them had eluded the scouts and murdered a family some distance down the river. A company was formed and started in pursuit of them. When they overtook them they were just ready for a war dance. They had some whites they had captured tied to a stake and were ready to set them afire. A number of them were killed - but most of them ran into the brush and escaped, as it was getting dark and pursuit was out of the question.

There was one incident that took place there that Granpap never forgot - or rather - never got over. There was a man by the name of Dunbar - a Frenchman - who was right by the side of Granpap when they charged the camp. A squaw had left her little papoose in the teepe. Dunbar saw it. He grabbed it up and dashed its brains out against a tree.
    Granpap saw him do it and he was so enraged that he rushed upon Dunbar and would have brained him with his tomahawk, but a man named Corbin sprange in between them.
    He never forgave Dunbar. His eyes would flash with indignation whenever he spoke of it.

I will relate one more incident that took place west of the Monongahela river. I relate it from the fact it was the last invasion the Indians made in that country. A man named Corbin was an early settler on Whitly Creek. For the protection of his family and the few neighbors who lived near by, they built a large strong fort and surrounded it with a heavy stockade.

The Indians took this as an offence and determined to kill Corbin and his family. They made a number of attacks upon it but were repulsed with heavy losses. This enraged them and they determined to have revenge.

In the meantime, settlers had come in fast. The Americans had taken possession of Fort Duquesne (now Pittsburg) and the Indians' means of obtaining supplies were cut off. They were compelled to take refuge west of the Ohio river, and for two years there had been no signs of Indians, and the whites had become a little careless as to scouting. They depended on a class of men called hunters, and they were not much better than the Indians.

Three Indians eluded the scouts - came to Whitly creek and camped on top of the hill, across the creek where they could have a clear view of Corbin's house and grounds around it. They could see him at work, but he always carried his gun and they were afraid to attack him. How long they were there, no one knows, for they had sunk a hole in the ground so they could make a fire and not be seen.

Corbin was a Baptist preacher. A small log church had been built and on this Sunday morning he and his family - a wife two daughters and a son - started to church. When the Indians saw them coming thro' the clearing and Corbin not armed - now was the time. They could pass down the hill - cross the creek - go up through the brush without Corbin seeing them. They had gone some distance from the house, when he discovered he had forgotten his hymn book and turned back to get it. As he came out of the house he heard three guns crack - well he knew what that meant.

He grabbed his gun and called to his large savage dog to "go". He could hear the screams of the boy - one Indian had shot at him and missed, but the mother and oldest girl were killed. The youngest girl hid in the brush. The boy with his hatchet and dog were holding the Indian at bay, when Corbin came running toward them. The Indian turned and ran, and just as he came to the bush where the girl was hiding - she - thinking the Indian had gone - stepped out, and he scalped her and made his escape.

The girl was not seriously hurt, but the wound in her scalp never healed. The alarm was given and in a few hours a posse' was on their trail. They followed them as long as they could see, hopeing to overtake them before they got to the river, but they were just a minute too late. They were across and out of range of the guns. Granpap had a long range gun and he was one of the pursuing party. One of the Indians stood there patting on the seat of his pants. "He laid down and the others carried him away" was the way Granpap used to tell it.

I have been particular in relating this, for as I said, it was the last time that the Indians attempted to invade that country. I have seen the old church and gone to meeting there - have also seen the old fort and the graves of the Corbin family.

I do not know as this will be of enough interest for you to read it, but I wanted to tell you of these two incidents, to give you some idea of how our forefathers had to contend with the relentless savages. But he has gone and the white man is in his place, enjoying the fruits of the toil and privation of the early settler of our won - derful country.

They had little idea of what they were doing, or the foundation they were laying for what has followed.

IV

Itwas about 1802 or 1803 when Granpap came to the backwoods, but on his arrival, he and his
   wife and baby took up their abode in the Swerengen fort. It was built by a company of
   men that came from Maryland, or the western part of what is now Maryland -and it was
   built the same as all the other forts, and in the summer time the families had to
   take refuge there.

They were of Scotch-Irish descent and came from northern Ireland on account of religious
   persecution. They were Protestants (Presbyterians) and the names of some of them were
   Neil (Neal) - Kilpatric - Gilkey and Swerengen.

When Granpap got there with his little colony - Blossers - Keggys and Bairds - it made quite
   an addition to the little fort, and they were more than glad to receive them.
      The women and children were compelled to keep within the stockade or near it.
   The men were divided into squads - scouts and choppers. The choppers cutting down the
   timber and clearing up the land. The stock consisted of horses cows and sheep - which
   had to be brought into the stockade every night for fear of the Indians.

My Granmother Neil (my mother was Delilah Neal - her father was Wm Neil and her mother was
   Delilah (McClure) Neil) was either born in the fort or came there when a very small
   child, for her earliest reccolections were connected with it. The old fort was about
   all gone when I came on the scene of action - but the old men and women were there
   to tell their experiences of the early days.

I often heard my father say the only way he would know when Sunday came, his mother would
   make coffee for breakfast. Occasionaly a preacher would come along and preach a
   sermon or two for them.

I went to school in the same old log school house my father learned his letters in. It was
   an old delapidated house when I went to school in it - the seats were made out of
   what they called puncheons - trees split- smoothed off a little and legs put on - no
   backs. What would the children do now if they had to sit on that kind of seats, from
   eight to twelve and one to four, without any intermission?

The teacher sat on a high stool with a long stick, convenient to use on the most trifling
   occasion. But it was not long untill the Free School System was adopted - but not till
   after a long fight - and then our schools were all right. The little log school house
   served its day - such men as Lincoln, Buchanan and Blaine and many others got their
   start in the little log school house.

I have often wished those relics of the past had been preserved -the old forts - and old
   churches - so that we could now look on them. What a curiosity they would be. But
   the people who built them, were glad enough to get better, and when they got out of
   them, they were let go to decay. I think, that hardly a man could be found, who could
   tell where Fort Swerengen was located, or, in fact, knows there was such a place.

The Clemmer family has been represented in every war the United States has been engaged in-
   except the war with Spain - I am not sure whether any of our relatives were in it or
   not. Mike Clemmer was killed at Cold Harbor in the grand charge on the 18" of
   June 1864. I was in the same dreadful charge.
   ***************************************************************************************

SUPPLEMENT
      The following grandsons of Dr Joseph Neal Clemmer were in the World War.
      Jeremiah Staley - son of George G Clemmer
      John Wm Blaine - son of Mrs Libbie (Clemmer) Calvert
      Daniel Webster -    "   "   "          "          "
      Robert Glenn - son of Joseph N Clemmer
      Julius Neal -    "   "   "      "      "
      Joseph Neal - son of George G Clemmer - was in France in Y M C A work.

Genealogy of Joseph Neal and Elizabeth Ann Clemmer

Joseph Neal Clemmer -oldest son of Jasper and Delilah (Neil) Clemmer -was born Aug 22 1826
    Springhill Twp Fayette Co Pa. He had four brothers and one sister. He died at the home
    home of his oldest son - Wm Jasper - Clarksville Ia Apr 15 1902 age 75yr 7mo 23da.
    He is buried at Clarksville Ia.
    He married Elizabeth Ann Zerley (dau of Saml & Kizzy (Griffith) Zerley) Oct 21 1847
    in the old Gans Home in Fayette Co Pa not far from Smithfield on the road from
    Fairchance to the old Clemmer home where Joseph Neal was born.(In 1907 the writer
    visited both the old Gans and Clemmer farms and the same houses were occupied) The
    house where Joseph Neal was born was built in 1826.

    Elizabeth Ann Zerley- was born in Fayette Co Pa Dec 10 1828. She had four brothers and four
    sisters. Her father died when she was twelve years old, and her mother two years later.
        She then made her home with the Joseph Gans family till she was married. She died at
    Whiting Ia Dec 2 1889 - age 60yr 11mo 22da. Buried at Whiting Ia in the Harrison
    cemetery four miles southwest of town.

    J N and his wife left Pa for Green Co Wis in the spring of 1848 with a colony and settled on
    a farm west of Juda not far from the big spring. Lydia Jane was born there. They moved
    on a farm between Juda and Brodhead- where Mary Louise was born. Next move they made
    was on land in Sylvester Twp - bought of the gov't- known as the uncle John Chryst farm-
    where Kate was born.

    In the spring of 1852 he went to Pa and studied medicine under old Dr Clemmer- later going to
    Cincinnati Ohio and entering the Eclectic College, then to Rush Medical College Chicago.
        He began the practice of his profession in Argyle LaFayette Co Wis, where he remained
    for three years. Here Wm Jasper was born. He then went to Decorah Iowa and two years later
    to Juda Green Co Wis. They lived in town in what is known as the Chadwick house, where
    Nettie was born. George G was Born in Decorah.

    He enlisted in the war of the Rebellion Mar 9 1863 and served till July 26 1865. He was
    promoted to regimental commissary and was in fourteen battles; serving in the second
    corps second division 1" Brigade Army of the Potomac; Gen'l Hancock commander of corps,
    and was mustered out at Jeffersonville Indiana.

    While Dr Clemmer was away to war, his wife and children moved to the place just east of the
    railway station at Juda and continued to live there till March 1886- when they moved to
    Whiting Iowa. In the summer following his wife's death- Dec 2 1889- Dr Clemmer sold his
    practice at Whiting and located at Clarksville Ia where he carried on his profession
    till his death - Apr 15 1902.

        Family line up to 1924. Names of deceased in red letters

I-- Lydia Jane b Sept 22 1848 Juda Wis m Wilbur R Shafer Dec 22 1865 Brodhead Wis
    Died Clarksville Ia Feb 25 1917 age 68yr 5mo 3da. Buried at Clarksville Ia.

    1- Lena Lydia Leora b Dec 21 1866 m John K Gabby Apr 27 1892
        d Apr 28 1904 age 57yr 4mo 7da. Buried Clarksville Ia

        a-Galen Eugene b June 26 1900 res Osage Ia

    2-Nettie Alpharetta b May 1 1868 m Grant Moulton (June 9 1909) Nov 21 1887
    res Fargo North Dakota

        a-Zelma b Sept 7 1891 m Dr J E Martin June 30 1916

        b-Helen b Apr 20 1895 m Grant L Martin Sept 15 1921

        c- Minota b May 24 1905 died at birth

Lydia Jane - continued

3-Thomas Jefferson b Oct 6 1869 m Fennie F Owens Jan 21 1891
    res Clarksville Ia

4-Mary Anna Dell b Nov 21 1874 m John M Ramsey Sept 30 1893
    res Clarksville Ia

        a-Georgia Edna b Mar 20 1900 m Gay Jackson June 24 1915
           res Clarksvil'e Ia

                (1)John James b Mar 2 1919
                     d Apr 26 1919 age 1mo 24da

                (2)Robert Gay b Dec 16 1921

                (3)

        b-Alice Lavon b Oct 15 1906

5-George Creighton b Apr 27 1877 d Jan 8 1910 age 32yr 8mo 11da

6-Fred L b Oct 2 1879 m Minone Darnell May 2 1905 res New Hampton Ia

        a-Yosonda Fredene b Aug 31 1908

7-Victor Ruloff b Dec 17 1882 m Janet King
    res Clarksville Ia

        a-Faye Catherine b Oct 10 1907

        b-Alice Janet b Nov 22 1913

8-Celia Inez b Apr 29 1887 m Wm J Gunther Mar 1902
    m Clyde C Newman Aug 21 1911 res Ocean Cove Cal

        a-Lydia Lorena Gunther b Sept 7 1903

9-Alice Luella b June 17 1889 m Claire H Rhodes
    res Clarksville Ia

        a-Miller Reid b Mar 15 1915

        b-Raymond Drexel b Feb 15 1917

II— Mary Louise b July 6 1850 Juda Wis m Geo H Brooks (Aug 17 1922) July 30 1865 at
Brodhead Wis.   Died at Whiting Ia July 14 1918 age 68yr 8da.
Geo H Brooks married Mrs Jane Fetterly May 22 1919.
Geo and Louise Brooks went to Monona Co Ia from Juda Wis in the autumn of 1868,
making the journey with an ox team and settled on a farm in Lincoln Twp west of
Whiting where they continued to reside till 1902 — when they moved to Onawa Ia and
later to Whiting Ia. He was struck by a passing automobile and seriously injured,
dying the next day. Both are buried in the Harrison cemetery southwest of Whiting.

1-William Jasper b Sept 20 1867 Juda Wis m Edith E Cutler Apr 12 1893
res Whiting Ia

a-Zelma Louise b Sept 30 1895 res Whiting Ia

b-Geo Cutler b Sept 16 1900 m Alice E Smith Nov 10 1921
res Whiting Ia

c-Edith Eila b Aug 14 1913

2-Geo Warren  b Mar 26 1871 d Aug 27 1872 age 1yr 5mo 1da

3-Percy Neal  b Mar 4 1880 d Aug 17 1880 age 5mo 13da

4-Lloyd Ullen b Nov 20 1881 m Cordilla Potter Nov 11 1901 Whiting Ia
d Franklin Neb Oct 18 1903 age 21yr 10mo 18da. Buried Whiting Ia

a-Charles Edward b Mar 14 1903 res Manning Ia

5-Geo Roy b May 21 1883 m Rose Adell Hawkins Sept 18 1907 res Whiting Ia

a- Infant b Jan 15 1909 d Jan 21 1909 age 6da

b-Ruth Adell b Nov 6 1910

c-Mable Louise b Oct 11 1913

d-Gail Dean b Mar 13 1916

6-Infant b Aug 27 1888 d Sept 11 1888 age 14da

7- Victor Neal  b Dec 5 1890 d Jan 19 1891 age 1mo 14da

III--Isabel Cathrine (Kate) b May 20 1852 Juda Wis m Geo W Scott  Mar 18 1874 Brodhead Wis
m Judson Munger Feb 21 1886 Monroe Wis res Onawa Ia.
Judson Munger died in Brodhead Wis Mar 17 1911 from injuries received in a
runaway, when breaking horses a few days before.

1-James Walter Scott  b Mar 26 1875 d Mar 5 1879 age 3ye 11mo 9da

2- Louezetta b Nov 3 1876 d Juda Wis Jan 16 1878 age 1yr 2mo 13da

3-Bertha Louella B Feb 20 1879 Juda Wis m Dr Rush R Gingles Castana Ia
Oct 7 1897 res Onawa Ia

a-Edna Elizabeth b Feb 3 1901 Seattle Washington
m Clarence J Thurston Onawa Ia Oct 30 1922

b-Aileen Lucile b May 18 1912 Onawa Ia

IV--William Jasper   b Apr 9 1854 Argyle Wis m Mary E A(Nettie)Shafer (sister of Wilbur R)
Nov 5 1876 Clarksville Ia. Died July 22 1918- 8days after his sister Louise passed
away- age 64yr 3mo 13da. He went to Clarksville Ia from Juda Wis when a young man
and married there - living on a farm till his death - and is buried by the side of
his father - Dr J N Clapper.

1-Tolbert Alonzo b Aug 6 1877 Clarksville Ia m Jennie June Dicky
res Belle Plaine Ia

a-William Avery b Nov 19 1904

b-Neal Ellsworth b Sept 12 1906

c-Alice Marguerite b Jan 6 1909

d-Beverly Nell b Jan 12 1913

2-Nellie b Jan 24 1880 m Harry Cook July 6 1899 res Clarksville Ia

a- Roy b Nov 13 1902 d Dec 10 1902 age 25da

b-Alonzo Harry b Nov 24 1904

c-Dorla Ruth b Oct 14 1906

V--George Gans b Jan 11 1857 Decorah Ia m Evelyn Mackey  (Jan 17 1881) Sept 1 1878 Juda Wis

1-Goldie Oct 10 1880 d Jan 15 1881 age 3mo 5da. His wife and baby are buried in
the same casket in Mt Vernon cemetery Juda Wis. In the employ of the
C M and St Paul Ry at Monroe Wis Feb 1886, he suffered the loss of his left leg. He
is employed by the company as stationary engineer (1924) and lives at Ferguson Ia.
Married May Sullivan July 23 1882 Monroe Wis.

1-Clarence Lee b June 6 1883 Monroe Wis m Helen Hoffman Oct 13 1913
res South Sioux City Neb

a-Marjorie Kathryn b July 20 1914 Omaha Neb

2-Joseph Neal b Apr 2 1885 Monroe Wis m Chloe M Cook June 6 1916
res Nevada Ia

a-Dorothy Lucile b May 2 1917

b-J Neal Jr b May 14 1919 d Dec 22 1920 age 1yr 7mo 8da

c-Craig Cook b Oct 21 1922

3-Edna May b July 11 1887 m Andrew Murphy Apr 27 1910 Sioux City Ia
m Geo John Schreck Feb 12 1921 Ferguson Ia res Welch West Virginia

a-Geo Theodore b Apr 3 1922 Camp Lewis Seattle Wn
d Apr 6 1922 age 3da

b-Frances Marie b Apr 14 1923 Camp Lewis Seattle Wn

4-George Dell b July 12 1889 Braymer Mo m Alma Anderson Dec 24 1911
Sioux City Ia
m Gertrude Harrington July 28 1916
res 3786 Hazlewood Ave Detroit Mich

a-Della May b Aug 23 1919

5-Jeremiah Staley b Jan 24 1892 Elwood Ia m Velma Deane Lewis Apr 21 1920
res Taintor Ia

a-Betty May b Feb 25 1921 Ferguson Ia

b-Robert Bruce b Nov 1 1922 Ferguson Ia

V--Geo Gans- continued

      6-Dorothy Elizabeth b Aug 26 1893 Elwood Ia
          m Charles B Duffy Aug 9 1912 res Granger Ia

          a-Jack b May 14 1913

      7-Evelyn Irene b June 23 1895 Coon Rapids Ia
          m Benj F Haffner July 20 1915 res Sabula Ia

      8-Theodore Hewitt b May 18 1897 Coon Rapids Ia res Ferguson Ia

      9-Frances Sullivan b Sept 29 1900 Coon Rapids Ia
          m John A Miller Jan 14 1920 res Des Moines Ia

      10-Julius Bruce b Sept 29 1904 Coon Rapids Ia res Ferguson Ia

VI-- Delilah Annetta (Nettie) b Jan 8 1861 Juda Wis m Robt S Tennyson Dec 30 1886
      Clarksville Ia. Died July 18 1919 age 58yr 6mo 10da.  She went to Clarksville Ia
      from Juda Wis in 1885 - where she married and lived on a farm till her death.
      She is buried at Clarksville.

      1-Mable Elizabeth b Sept 18 1889 m Vernal Moore (Mar 8 1921) Jan 27 1916
          res Clarksville Ia

          a-Alta Lucile Moore b Feb 20 1917

      2-Erma b Aug 9 1896 m DeLoss Polk Mar 26 1919 res Cedar Falls Ia

          a-Robert Harold  b Feb 5 1920 d July 16 1920 age 5mo 11da
          b-Arthur Fredrick b Sept 20 1921

      3-Joseph William b Feb 2 1899 res Clarksville Ia

VII--Anna Dell(Della) b Mar 30 1857 Juda Wis m Julius T Cutter July 8 1891 Castana Ia
      She went to Whiting Ia from Juda Wis in March 1886. Res Castana Iowa.

VIII
&
IX-- Joseph Neal and Elizabeth Ann -twins

Joseph Neal b July 10 1870 Juda Wis m Laura May Cox Apr 18 1893 Castana Ia. He went to
Whiting Ia with his parents in the spring of 1886. Res Omaha Neb.

      1-Raymond Earl b <u>may</u> Mar 7 1894 Castana Ia
        m Genevieve Farley Feb 12 1917 res 4129 S St South Omaha Neb

        a-Joseph Darrel b Dec 28 1922 St Josephs Hospital

      2-Robert Glenn b Aug 12 1896 Castana Ia
        m Roseanna Miljure Dec 23 1921 Mitchell So Dakota
        res Sioux Falls So Dak

      3-Julius Neal b June 21 1899 Castana Ia
        m Colinette Lear May 4 1921 Omaha Neb res 3411 Taylor St Omaha Neb

        a-Betty May b Dec 12 1921 Denver Colo

        b-J Neal b Jan 26 1923 Omaha Neb

Elizabeth Ann(bibbie) b July 10 1870 Juda Wis m J W Calvert May 30 1886 Whiting Ia. She
went to Whiting Ia with her parents in the spring of 1886. Res 602 Iowa Ave North
Washington Ia.

      1-Mable Elizabeth b Aug 28 1887 Haverhill Ia m Arthur McCammon
        Apr 12 1904 res Miles City Mont Pine Hills Route

        a-Joseph Wm McCammon b Nov 20 1904 res Mystic Ia

      2-Hazle May b Oct 25 1889 Polo Mo m Earl Jones Jan 1 1909 Mystic Ia
        res New Town Mo

        a-Calvert Claude b Nov 3 1909 Powersville Mo

        b-Robert Elmer b Oct 11 1912 Mystic Ia

        c-Fremont Earl b Jan 22 1916 Powersville Mo

        d-Margaret Elizabeth b June 17 1920 New Town Mo

Elizabeth Ann- continued

       3-John Wm Blaine b Jan 2 1893 Lawson Mo m Therese Oliver Jan 7 1920 Borough Hall
          Brooklyn New York res 1139 Division St Ottumwa Ia

              a-Jack Wm Bernard b May 28 1923


       4-Blanche Lavina b May 24 1895 Seymour Ia m Ray E Dingeman Sept 7 1917
          Knoxville Ia res Fort Eustic Virginia

              a-David Ray b July 22 1919 Presisio San Francisco Cal

              b-Beth Louise b Dec 23 1920 Presidio San Francisco Cal

              c-Robert Edward b June 12 1922 Fort Mills Corregidor
                  Phillipine Islands


       5-Daniel Webster b Feb 25 1897 Mystic Ia res Miles City Mont Pine Hills Route


       6-Sadie Adelaide b July 17 1899 Mystic Ia res Washington Ia


       7-Major Clemmer b May 15 1902 Mystic Ia res Washington Ia


       8-Reta Zerley b Oct 24 1912 Mystic Ia res Washington Ia

Jasper Clemmer b York Co Pa June 16 1801. Died Dec 17 1885 Juda Wis age 84yr 6mo 1da
Delilah Neal (Neil) b Pa Sept 13 1805. Died Dec 21 1887 Cresco Ia at the home of her son
    Jacob Jefferson - age 82yr 4mo 8da. Both are buried in Mt Vernon cemetery
    Juda Wis.
Married Oct 13 1825 Fayette Co Pa

    1--Joseph Neal m Elizabeth Ann Zerley res Juda Wis

    2-James Witter m Jane Roderick res Juda Wis

    3-Minerva Jane m John Chryst res Juda Wis

    4-John Andrew m Rhoda Whitcomb (d Dec 4 1921) res Monroe Wis

    5-Jacob Jefferson m Phoeba Thornburg res Cresco Ia

    6-George Gans m Elizabeth Johnson res Hampton Ia


Samuel Zerley b Fayette Co Pa May 22 1803. Died Oct 29 1840 Smithfield Pa age 37yr 5mo 7da
Kaziah (Kizzy) Griffith b Fayette Co Pa Apr 6 1807. Died May 10 1842 Smithfield Pa
    age 35yr 1mo 4da.
Married 1823.

    1-William m Mary Husted - m Caroline Joliff res Fairchance Pa

    2-Levi G m Elizabeth Moore res Liberty Center Warren Co Ia

    3-Simeon m Rebecca Burchnell res Monroe Ia

    4-Elizabeth Ann m Joseph Neal Clemmer res Juda Wis

    5-Cathrine d Fayette Co Pa age 16yr - July 18 1847

    6-John T d Fayette Co Pa age 1yr

    7-Mary Anna (d June 6 1911) m Justice Dunn res Fairchance Pa

    8-Sarah Jane m James Nixon res Fairchance Pa

    9-Leah Lavina m Ferdinand Willits res Chicago Ill

******************************************

Compiled and arranged by Mrs Della Clemmer Cutter Castana Iowa

# Annex B
# Awards & Diplomas

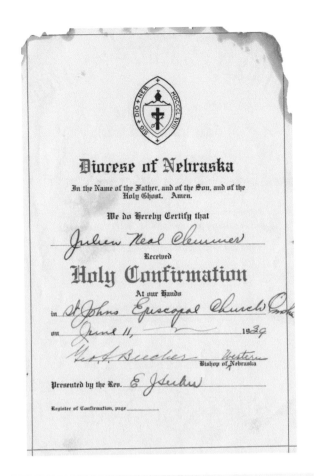

# Diocese of Nebraska

In the Name of the Father, and of the Son, and of the
Holy Ghost. Amen.

We do Hereby Certify that

*Julius Neal Clemmer*

Received

# Holy Confirmation

At our Hands

in *St. Johns Episcopal Church Omaha*

on *June 11,* 19*39*

*Geo. A. Beecher* Western
Bishop of Nebraska

Presented by the Rev. *E. J. Suhr*

Register of Confirmation, page _____

---

# OMAHA PUBLIC SCHOOLS

## HIGH SCHOOL DEPARTMENT

THIS

# DIPLOMA

CERTIFIES THAT

## Julius Neal Clemmer, Jr.

HAS BEEN A MEMBER OF THE NORTH
HIGH SCHOOL AND HAS SATISFACTORILY COM-
PLETED A FOUR YEAR COURSE PRESCRIBED
BY THE BOARD OF EDUCATION OF THE SCHOOL
DISTRICT OF OMAHA, NEBRASKA.

GIVEN BY AUTHORITY OF THE BOARD OF EDU-
CATION OF THE SCHOOL DISTRICT OF OMAHA
THIS SIXTH DAY OF JUNE, A. D. NINETEEN
HUNDRED FORTY-ONE.

PRESIDENT                    E. E. McMillan
                             PRINCIPAL

Mary E. Bird
SECRETARY                    H. M. Corning
                             SUPERINTENDENT OF SCHOOLS

# UNITED STATES ARMY

### 9th Army Air Force
### Flying Training Detachment

**Be It Known That**   Julius N. Clemmer

United States Army, has satisfactorily completed the
course of instruction for *PRIMARY PILOT TRAINING*.

In testimony whereof, there is conferred upon him this

## DIPLOMA

Given at Fort Stockton, Texas, this 29th day of July, in the
year of our Lord one thousand nine hundred and forty-three.

_____
Director of Flying

_____          _____
Commandant of Cadets                      Commanding

---

# United States Army

### KEY FIELD REPLACEMENT TRAINING UNIT
### TACTICAL RECONNAISSANCE

Be it known that  *Julius N. Clemmer, 2d Lieut., ASN O 707 660*

United States Army, has satisfactorily completed the course of

instruction prescribed for *tactical Reconnaissance Pilot Training.*

In testimony whereof and by virtue of vested authority I do

confer upon him this

## ——— DIPLOMA ———

Given at *Key Field, Meridian, Mississippi,* this       2d       day

of       *August*       in the year of our Lord one thousand

nine hundred and *forty-four.*

attest:

_____
Lt. Colonel, Air Corps,
Commanding Officer.

_____          _____
Major, Air Corps,                         Lt. Colonel, Air Corps,
Adjutant.                                        Director of Training.

# The Iowa State College
## of Agriculture and Mechanic Arts
*hereby confers upon*

### Julius Neal Clemmer
*the Degree of*

## Bachelor of Science
*with all the Honors and Distinctions belonging to this Degree in consideration of the satisfactory completion of the Course of Study prescribed in*

## Agronomy
*Given at Ames, Iowa on the nineteenth day of March in the year of our Lord one thousand nine hundred and forty-nine*

_Henry C. Shull_
President of the Iowa State Board of Education

_Lances E. _____
President of the College

---

# United States Air Force

## Air Training Command

Be it known that 1ST LT JULIUS N. CLEMMER        AO 707660

has satisfactorily completed the prescribed course of instruction of the

Air Training Command specializing in

        AIRCRAFT CONTROLLER        AFSC 1631

In testimony whereof and by virtue of vested authority we do confer upon

him this

## ═══ CERTIFICATE OF PROFICIENCY ═══

Given at USAF Aircraft Controllers School, Tyndall Air Force Base, Florida

on this        fourth        day of        August

in the year of our Lord one thousand nine hundred and   fifty-two

Attest:

_George J. Frey_
GEORGE J. FREY
Captain, USAF
SECRETARY

_B. T. Kleine_
B. T. KLEINE
Colonel, USAF
COMMANDANT

## UNITED STATES AIR FORCE
### AIR TRAINING COMMAND

#### Completion of Training
#### Certificate

This is to certify that

1ST LT JULIUS N CLEMMER    AO 707660

has satisfactorily completed an approved training program in

the doctrine of Tactical Air Controlling

consisting of          forty-three          hours of instruction.

Given at   USAF Aircraft Controllers School, Tyndall Air Force Base, Florida

on this     eighteenth     day of   August

in the year of our Lord one thousand nine hundred and   fifty-two

Attest:

GEORGE J. FREY
Captain, USAF
School Secretary

DANIEL A. SIMS
Lt Colonel, USAF
COMMANDING

C1-1481--AF-Chanute AFB, Ill. 6-19-51 45M

---

## Air University
# Extension Course Institute

### United States Air Force

Be it known that   1st Lt Julius N Clemmer  AO 707660   is a graduate of the

Squadron Officer Correspondence Course, Air Command & Staff School

In testimony whereof, and by authority vested in us, we do confer upon him this

## Diploma

Given at Gunter Air Force Base, Alabama, this 30 day of   October   , 1953

Commandant

W H Frederick
Air University Secretary

Commander, Air University

Director of Education

USAF-GAFB, ALA (DJ1205)/440

UNITED STATES AIR FORCE

## AIR-GROUND OPERATIONS SCHOOL

Be it known that

CAPTAIN JULIUS N. CLEMMER, AO707660

Has successfully completed the course of
instruction prescribed for

The Indoctrination Course

In testimony whereof, and by virtue of
vested authority I do confer upon him
this

### ⇝ Diploma ⇜

Given at Southern Pines, North Carolina
this 9th day of December in the year of our
lord one thousand nine hundred and fifty-
five.

D. W. JENKINS
BRIGADIER GENERAL U.S.A.F.
Commandant

ALFRED K. CLARK
COLONEL U.S.A.
Deputy Commandant

Attest
Lieutenant Colonel U.S.A.F.
EXECUTIVE OFFICER

Air Force LAFB-L-4-1178

---

## THE RAND CORPORATION
## SANTA MONICA, CALIFORNIA

⇉⇉⇉⇉⇇⇇⇇⇇

# CERTIFICATE
# OF PROFICIENCY

⇉⇉⇉⇉⇇⇇⇇⇇

this certifies that

JULIUS N. CLEMMER    CAPT    USAF

has demonstrated
instructor proficiency in radar-scope interpretations
and air mass-positioning techniques
in simulated multiple-interceptor control

APRIL 13, 1956
date

chief instructor

## THE AMERICAN RED CROSS
### ROANOKE RAPIDS-LITTLETON CHAPTER
### ROANOKE RAPIDS, N. C.

May 20, 1957

Captain J.N. Clemmer
632nd ACW Sqdn.
Roanoke Rapids Air Force Base
Roanoke Rapids, North Carolina.

Dear Captain Clemmer:

This is to express our appreciation to you for speaking to the regional meeting of the American Red Cross Tidewater Region Blood Center held in Hampton, Virginia on Tuesday April 30, 1957. Your ability to speak so effectively on the subject -- "How to Make a Bloodmobile Visit a Successful Community Project" -- based on your own personal experience and that of so many of your associates at the Air Force Installation in Roanoke Rapids is another clear indication of the extent each of you and your unit is participating in local community projects -- projects from which not only your own personnel benefits but projects from which the remainder of the community and this area benefit to a much greater extent.

I enjoyed the trip down and back with you and please let me say again that our best wishes go with you when you leave shortly for a new assignment.

Yours sincerely,

William C. Thompson
Chapter Chairman.

WCT/nls

---

## THE AMERICAN NATIONAL RED CROSS
### NATIONAL HEADQUARTERS
### WASHINGTON 13, D. C.

OFFICE OF THE PRESIDENT

May 23, 1957

Dear Captain Clemmer:

One of the major ways in which the American Red Cross is privileged to serve the American people is through the Blood Program. The success of the Red Cross in providing more than two million pints a year rests solely on the efforts of the men and women throughout the country who recruit donors.

In all of the "success stories" that have been told to me since I came to the Red Cross, I know of none more worthy of commendation than your efforts in recruiting donors at Roanoke Rapids, North Carolina. I understand that, as a direct result of your publicity efforts, 266 pints of blood were collected on a recent visit of a blood mobile to your Base, which was exactly 200 pints more than had been collected at the previous visit and was the largest amount ever collected in the history of the Roanoke Rapids-Littleton Chapter.

You have my hearty congratulations and very great appreciation.

Sincerely,

Alfred M. Gruenther

Captain Julius Neal Clemmer
632nd Aircraft Control and
Warning Squadron
Roanoke Rapids, N. C.

68

# Department of the Air Force

## CERTIFICATE OF TRAINING

*This is to certify that*

CAPTAIN JULIUS N CLEMMER, AO 707660

*has satisfactorily completed the*

GUIDANCE SYSTEMS OFFICER (SURFACE TO SURFACE)(TM-61C) COURSE

## Given by

3415TH TECHNICAL TRAINING WING, LOWRY AIR FORCE BASE, COLORADO

14 JANUARY 1958

E P MUSSETT
MAJOR GENERAL, USAF

AF FORM 1256, 1 JAN 55                                    GPO:1955 O - 332252

---

# AIR FORCE BALLISTIC MISSILE DIVISION

## HQ,ARDC

*This Certifies that*

CAPTAIN J. CLEMMER

*has attended*

## BALLISTIC MISSILE INDOCTRINATION COURSE

*conducted at*

AIR FORCE BALLISTIC MISSILE DIVISION
HEADQUARTERS, AIR RESEARCH AND DEVELOPMENT COMMAND
INGLEWOOD, CALIFORNIA

FROM 24 February 1958 TO 28 February 1958

B. A. SCHRIEVER
MAJ. GEN., USAF
COMMANDER

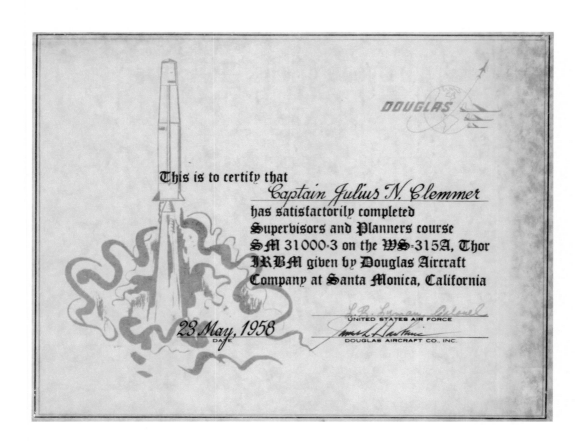

This is to certify that

*Captain Julius N. Clemmer*

has satisfactorily completed
Supervisors and Planners course
SM 31000-3 on the WS-315A, Thor
IRBM given by Douglas Aircraft
Company at Santa Monica, California

23 May, 1958
DATE

UNITED STATES AIR FORCE

DOUGLAS AIRCRAFT CO., INC.

## CERTIFICATE OF TRAINING
### ON THE
## THOR WEAPON SYSTEM

This is to certify that

CAPTAIN JULIUS N. CLEMMER

has satisfactorily completed a course of training
as indicated below in the United States Air Force
IRBM (Thor) Weapons System. This acknowledge-
ment is presented as a record of his proficiency in
the skills required to support this Air Frame and
Ground Support Equipment.

GUIDED MISSILE MAINTENANCE OFFICER - SM 3142B-1
COURSE NAME AND NUMBER

DOUGLAS AIRCRAFT CO., INC.

12 AUG 58
DATE

UNITED STATES AIR FORCE

# Department of the Air Force

## CERTIFICATE OF TRAINING

*This is to certify that*

CAPTAIN  JULIUS N CLEMMER  AO707660

*has satisfactorily completed the*

INTERIM INTEGRATED WEAPONS SYSTEM TRAINING  MAINTENANCE MANAGEMENT COURSE

*Given by*

392D MISSILE TRAINING SQUADRON  VANDENBERG AIR FORCE BASE  CALIFORNIA

ATTESTED  31 October 1958

ROBERT W CHRISTY
Colonel, USAF
Commander

MR. JOHN MAAS
Douglas Aircraft Company, Inc

AF FORM 1256, 1 JAN 55

GPO:1955 O - 532252

---

## AIR UNIVERSITY

*United States Air Force*

## EXTENSION COURSE INSTITUTE

Date  18 APR 1960

Be it known  CPT J N CLEMMER  AO0707660  is a graduate of

COMMAND AND STAFF COLLEGE  course  0003

in testimony whereof and by authority vested in us, this diploma
is hereby conferred. Given at Gunter Air Force Base, Alabama,
this day as dated above.

★ ★ ★ ★ ★

OFFICIAL

WILFRED W. WAGNER
Lt. Colonel, USAF
Commandant

WALTER E. TODD
Lieutenant General, USAF
Commander, Air University

FRANK D. HUTCHINS
Colonel, USAF
Air University Secretary

# 1st MISSILE DIVISION

## THIS IS TO CERTIFY THAT ★ ★ ★ ★

CAPTAIN JULIUS N. CLEMMER

Has on ___12 August 1960___ satisfactorily completed

— BALLISTIC MISSILE STAFF FAMILIARIZATION —

Training Course · ·

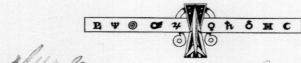

_dWade_
Major General, Commander
1st Missile Division

_John F. Watters, Lt Col USAF_
Commander

---

# Department of the Air Force

## CERTIFICATE OF TRAINING

_This is to certify that_

CAPTAIN JULIUS N. CLEMMER, AO-707660

_has satisfactorily completed the_

SPECIAL STAFF MISSILE MAINTENANCE MANAGEMENT COURSE AMF31000-1 (24 HOUR)

_Given by_

FIELD TRAINING DETACHMENT #15 3764TH SCHOOL SQUADRON (ATC)
VANDENBERG AIR FORCE BASE, CALIFORNIA          12 OCTOBER 1960

_Leonard N. Frindt_
LEONARD N. FRINDT, CAPT., OIC

_Raymond Coy_
RAYMOND W. COY, MAJOR, USAF
Commander, FTD #15

AF FORM 1256, 1 JAN 55

☆ GPO:1955 O - 332252

# Department of the Air Force

## CERTIFICATE OF TRAINING

### This is to certify that

CAPTAIN JULIUS N. CLEMMER, AO707660

### has satisfactorily completed the

MISSILE MAINTENANCE MANAGEMENT COURSE AMF31000-1  (80 HOURS)

### Given by

FIELD TRAINING DETACHMENT #15 3764TH SCHOOL SQUADRON (ATC)
VANDENBERG AIR FORCE BASE, CALIFORNIA        28 OCTOBER 1960

Leonard N. Frindt
LEONARD N. FRINDT, CAPT, OIC

RAYMOND W. COY, MAJOR, USAF
Commander, FTD #15

AF FORM 1256, 1 JAN 55                              ☆ GPO:1955 O - 332252

---

Ltr, 1 MD (DT), 23 Dec 60, Letter of Appreciation

1st Ind (392MTSC)                              28 Dec 60

392d Missile Training Squadron (IRBM), Vandenberg AFB, California

TO:  Captain Julius N. Clemmer, AO707660, 392d Missile Training Squadron
(IRBM), Vandenberg AFB, California

1.  It is always gratifying to receive letters such as this. From what
General Sweeney said it is obvious that the exercise mentioned was a
highly successful one.

2.  I would like to add my own thanks to those of Colonel Dowtin.
Your contribution to the success of Road Show was truly significant
and I am personally aware of the time and effort you expended in
making it a completely professional performance.


JOHN F. WATTERS
Lt Colonel, USAF
Commander

HEADQUARTERS
1ST MISSILE DIVISION (SAC)
UNITED STATES AIR FORCE
VANDENBERG AIR FORCE BASE, CALIFORNIA

REPLY TO
ATTN OF: C

12 May 1961

SUBJECT: Letter of Favorable Communication

TO: Captain Julius N. Clemmer
392 Msl Tng Sq
Vandenberg AFB, Calif

1. I want to take this opportunity to commend you for the outstanding contributions and efforts you have made in making the Ballistic Missile Staff Familiarization Course a highly successful tool in indoctrinating key staff personnel with a working knowledge of ballistic missiles and space vehicles.

2. From the time of its inception, this course has been attended by senior staff officers, not only from SAC but from all other commands throughout the Department of Defense. The Ballistic Missile Staff Familiarization Course has been universally praised and accepted as one of the most outstanding missile courses presented by the Air Force, and the volume of favorable comments received regarding the course administration, content, and professional manner of presentation is most gratifying. This commendatory appraisal reflects credit upon this headquarters, the Strategic Air Command, and the Air Force.

3. The success of this course is most certainly due to your aggressiveness, sincerity, and high degree of professional ability. For these efforts, I extend my sincerest gratitude for a job well done.

s/David Wade
t/DAVID WADE
Major General, USAF
Commander

A TRUE COPY

# 1ˢᵗ MISSILE DIVISION

## THIS IS TO CERTIFY THAT ★ ★ ★

CAPTAIN JULIUS N. CLEMMER

Has on __24 March 1961__ satisfactorily completed

STAFF OFFICERS FAMILIARIZATION COURSE (SM68 TITAN) 40 HOURS

## Training Course ··

Major General, Commander
1ˢᵗ Missile Division

Colonel, USAF
Commander
395TH MISSILE SQUADRON

# DEPARTMENT OF THE AIR FORCE

### THIS IS TO CERTIFY THAT

## THE AIR FORCE OUTSTANDING UNIT AWARD

### HAS BEEN AWARDED TO THE

392D MISSILE TRAINING SQUADRON (IRBM)

FROM 1 JANUARY 1958 TO 30 JUNE 1962

## AND

MAJOR JULIUS M. CLEMMER, AO707670

A MEMBER OF THIS UNIT DURING THE PERIOD FOR WHICH
THE AWARD WAS GRANTED IS ENTITLED TO
PERMANENTLY WEAR THE RIBBON REPRESENTING THIS AWARD

S. W. WELLS, Major General, USAF
Commander, 1st Strategic Aerospace Division

AF FORM 1096, 15 FEB 54

# DEPARTMENT OF THE AIR FORCE

### THIS IS TO CERTIFY THAT

## THE AIR FORCE COMMENDATION MEDAL

### HAS BEEN AWARDED TO

CAPTAIN JULIUS N. CLEMMER, AO707660

## FOR

MERITORIOUS SERVICE
3 February 1958 to 31 January 1963

GIVEN UNDER MY HAND IN THE CITY OF WASHINGTON
THIS    Fifteenth    DAY OF    March    1963

JOSEPH J. PRESTON, Major General, USAF
Commander, 1st Strategic Aerospace Division

Eugene M Zuckert
SECRETARY OF THE AIR FORCE

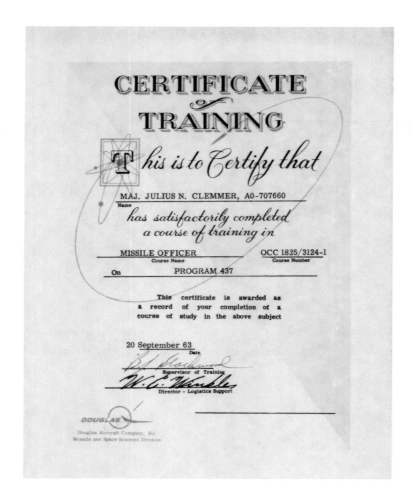

# CERTIFICATE of TRAINING

## This is to Certify that

MAJ. JULIUS N. CLEMMER, A0-707660
Name

### has satisfactorily completed
### a course of training in

MISSILE OFFICER                    OCC 1825/3124-1
Course Name                        Course Number

On              PROGRAM 437

This certificate is awarded as
a record of your completion of a
course of study in the above subject

20 September 63
Date

*B. J. Blackwood*
Supervisor of Training

*W. C. Wensley*
Director - Logistics Support

DOUGLAS

Douglas Aircraft Company, Inc.
Missile and Space Systems Division

---

# Department of the Air Force

## CERTIFICATE OF TRAINING

### This is to certify that

MAJOR JULIUS N. CLEMMER, A0707660

### has satisfactorily completed the

OCC 1825/3124-1, MISSILE OFFICER, TWO WEEKS

### Given by

DOUGLAS AIRCRAFT COMPANY, INC., 3000 OCEAN PARK BOULEVARD, SANTA MONICA, CALIFORNIA

20 September 1963

*B. J. Blackwood*

B. J. Blackwood
Supervisor - Training
MSSD - Douglas Aircraft Co.

AF FORM 1256. SEP 59                              * GPO : 1959 O—524415

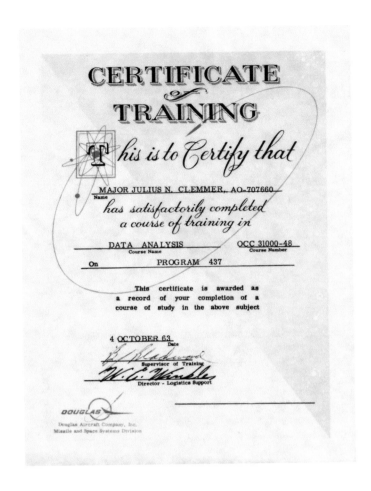

# CERTIFICATE
## of
# TRAINING

*This is to Certify that*

MAJOR JULIUS N. CLEMMER, AO-707660
Name

*has satisfactorily completed*
*a course of training in*

DATA ANALYSIS                    OCC 31000-48
Course Name                          Course Number

On            PROGRAM 437

This certificate is awarded as
a record of your completion of a
course of study in the above subject

4 OCTOBER 63
Date

Supervisor of Training

Director - Logistics Support

DOUGLAS

Douglas Aircraft Company, Inc.
Missile and Space Systems Division

---

# Department of the Air Force

# CERTIFICATE OF TRAINING

*This is to certify that*

MAJOR, JULIUS N. CLEMMER, AO-707660

## has satisfactorily completed the

OCC 31000-48 DATA ANALYSIS, THREE WEEKS

## Given by

DOUGLAS AIRCRAFT COMPANY, INC., 3000 OCEAN PARK BOULEVARD, SANTA MONICA, CALIFORNIA

4 October 1963

C. S. French
for

B. J. Blackwood
Supervisor - Training
MSSD - Douglas Aircraft Co.

AF FORM 1256. SEP 59                              GPO : 1959 O—524415

# Department of the Air Force

## CERTIFICATE OF TRAINING

*This is to certify that*

CAPTAIN JULIUS N. CLEMMER, AO707660

*has satisfactorily completed the*

SUPERVISORS AND PLANNERS, SM-80 COURSE (OTS31000-12)

*Given by*

3345TH TECHNICAL SCHOOL, USAF, CHANUTE AIR FORCE BASE, ILLINOIS

*Hadley B. Eliker*
HADLEY B. ELIKER
COLONEL, USAF
COMMANDER

7 DECEMBER 1962

AF FORM 1256. SEP 59

* GPO: 1959 O—524615

THE UNITED STATES AIR FORCE

*Certifies that*

MAJOR JULIUS N. CLEMMER, AO707660

*has successfully completed the*

ORBITAL MECHANICS COURSE ODF31000-7

*and is herewith awarded this*

CERTIFICATE of TRAINING

*Robert L. Walker*
ROBERT L. WALKER, Lt Col, USAF
Chief, Dept of Msl & Space Tng

27 August 1965
Date

AF FORM 1256. SEP 64

# Department of the Air Force

## CERTIFICATE OF TRAINING

*This is to certify that*

MAJOR JULIUS N. CLEMMER, FV707660

*has satisfactorily completed the*

DESIGN AND OPERATIONAL DATA (BURNER II) COURSE AMF 31000-10

*Given by*

FIELD TRAINING DETACHMENT #530S, 3774TH INSTRUCTOR SQUADRON (ATC), VANDENBERG AIR FORCE BASE, CALIFORNIA

4 February 1966

JAMES F. O'NEILL
Major, USAF
Commander

AF FORM 1256. SEP 59

* GPO. 1959 O—528415

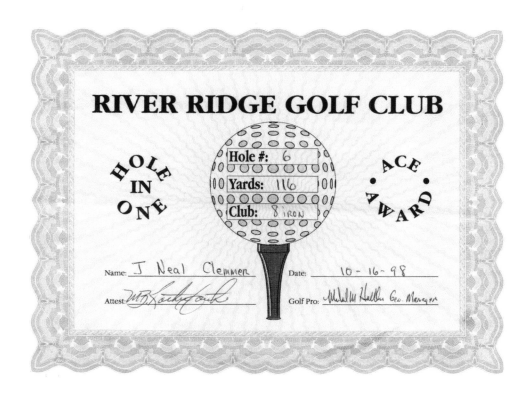